Endorsements

From a busy life to a hospital bed, fear and uncertainty are Heather MacAskill's lot. Her journey of highs and lows, despair and hope, captivate the reader.

One constant remains - her faith in God. Is it enough to fulfill her desires? This remarkable story kept me turning the pages. Heather has written a gripping tale that is a must-read.

Mary Haskett

Award-winning author of Reverend Mother's Daughter

maryhaskett.ca

During the most frightening and horrendous time of her life, in total surrender, God carried her through and she experienced the power, the kindness, the care of our Father, God Almighty in a personal and profound way. I highly recommend this book to nurture your soul. In a world where fear and lost hope seem omnipresent, we must remember that God is unmovable. He is the same today, the same yesterday and the same tomorrow. No life is without pain, but when we live it with God, that changes everything.

Louise Bélanger
Award-winning Author Your Words Collection
louisebelangerauthor.com

Heather MacAskill discovered the power of God's Word as she chewed on truths, meditated on their meaning, and processed the application to her life. This discipline came after a shocking brain tumor diagnosis that took her places mentally she had never experienced before. MacAskill piles Scripture upon Scripture as she wades through the mire of her ongoing cancer journey and comes out on the other side with a deeper trust in her Heavenly Father. Her open, raw approach shows us her pain and angst and how God's Word can lead us to a deeper faith in life's most difficult seasons. When she'd had enough, Heather discovered that He was enough. I recommend this story to anyone facing a life-threatening prognosis or someone walking alongside them.

Ruth Coghill
Speaker, Author of WOW Bible Study series,
Unborn. Untold. True Stories of Abortion and God's
Healing Grace

Enough

A Cancer Survivor's Journey from Protesting to Proclaiming

By Heather MacAskill

Abundance Books, LLC
Kalamazoo, MI

Enough

by

Heather MacAskill

Enough. A Cancer's Survivor's Journey From Protesting to Proclaiming.
ISBN 978-1-963377-04-0 (Print)
ISBN 978-1-963377-16-3 (E-book)

Published by
Abundance Books, LLC
Kalamazoo, Michigan

www.abundance-books.com

For my husband, Keith,
and our sons, Connor, Cameron, and Evan,
who stayed so close on this journey.

Contents

Prologue

Courage, dear heart.
C.S. Lewis

I'm an educator. I've spent many years teaching, and my first love was always grade seven and eight. This is an age where you either love 'em or lose your mind. I didn't plan to teach twelve- to fourteen-year-olds. When I first graduated, the school boards were practicing pool hiring. This was a process where they projected how many teaching positions they would have in the coming year and hired that many people. If successful, you had no idea what you would be teaching. I was just excited to have an actual job when I was hired. A few months later, I was standing in front of a grade seven class, wondering what in the world I was going to do. Doubt sat on my shoulder. Scanning the room, I felt bewildered with how I would connect with these teens. Their bored faces stared me down. God had obviously made a colossal mistake, because I was good with little kids, not these giants, some of whom were taller than me. By the end of the year, I understood the Lord's wisdom. I would not have picked it for myself, but I was utterly hooked on those students and that age group.

From that time on, I made a practice of listening to the Lord about what kind of job to take. I trusted him, and he led me on a path taking me to a couple of different school boards, many classes, and various positions. By the time I reached my fifties, I was in my dream position, teaching English to children new to Canada and students with special education needs. It was a position I never thought I would get because there weren't many openings, and I didn't have a lot of connections or seniority in this board. God worked it out, and I was offered the position at the school I was already in. So, to say I entered my fifties comfortable was an understatement. I loved what I did and knew it was a perfect fit.

In January 2019 I started to experience restlessness in my work. This was new, unexpected, and quite frankly, a little disturbing. Here I was with my dream job, and I was feeling unsatisfied. What was going on? Was I being ungrateful? I took the restlessness to God and laid out my questions. He had clearly orchestrated the position for me, so why was I dissatisfied? What was he up to? Was I missing something? I smile now when I think back to this time of questioning. It was an honesty before God that was sort of new to me. There had been experiences of difficulty and pain in my life, but this feeling of dissatisfaction was very foreign. I began to lean into my Scripture more, trying to discern what the Lord was doing.

That March, we planned to visit some family and friends on the school break. I was looking forward to getting away and connecting with those who lived far away. While I was packing to leave, God started to impress on me I should take a course for work. I had come across an email advertising courses to prepare for an administrative role, and I suddenly couldn't get it off my mind. God was clearly saying to me I should enroll. In my mind, God was obviously mistaken. I already had a job, one he had given me, and I loved it. There was no need for a change. I was not bilingual, so there was another reason why God was wrong. The city I lived in was highly bilingual, and school administrators needed to be able to communicate with everyone.

I had never seen myself as an administrator, didn't have a desire to be the person in charge. So, I laid out all of these reasons before the Lord and told him no. It didn't change his pursuit though. I kept packing for the trip, doing something to get my mind off the course. God started bringing to mind things that had been happening in the last couple of months. I had a new VP start at my school, and he wasn't bilingual. There were several colleagues, who I respected, who mentioned they thought I should pursue administration. I couldn't shake the feeling that my discontentment with my work was God-given. It was like God had already supplied all of the answers to my objections.

So, I did something I don't do a lot. I stopped. I quit packing, quieted my mind, and began to pray specifically about taking the course. I asked lots of questions. Questions about change, about his will for my work, about the necessity of it all. I also admitted the fear that came with taking this kind of risk. Being vulnerable before the Lord quieted my mind and created space for him to address the questions. It was surrendering a part of my will because I truly didn't want a change. In being still, I had to decide if I wanted God's will for my life or not, and if I would trust him enough with a direction I didn't choose. It was a struggle. It took releasing on my part of the need to control and the need to understand. When I got up from praying, I knew I would take the course.

Here's the part that causes a little shame. I didn't quite trust God completely. I gave a couple of conditions to my agreement. The course had a significant price tag attached, so I told God my husband would have to be comfortable with spending the money. Keith, my husband, barely blinked when I told him. His response was simply, "Well you better do it." So much for getting out of it that way! The other roadblock I had put up was the timing. The course was offered on weekends, which meant spending every other Sunday for several months at a course instead of at church. Surely after over twenty-five years in pastoral ministry, Keith would object. After all, I couldn't miss church! When I explained the timing, Keith paused briefly, then asked the question I didn't want to hear. "Are you confident God wants you to take this course?" I knew I was. "Well then you better do it."

God was so patient with me through the process. Yes, he had to basically smack me in the forehead to get my attention, but he kept pursuing until I submitted. I had to trust he had plans and purposes I didn't know about. It came down to this: Did I really believe he was God? If I did, then there wasn't any other option. I enrolled in the course. As soon as I hit submit on that enrollment form, a peace washed over me, and it was like Jesus looked me in the eyes, smiled lovingly, and said, "Now that wasn't so hard, was it?" He took my hand and began to lead me in a whole new direction.

I had no idea how pivotal that moment was. It would become a cornerstone in the building of my faith. God was giving me a direction change to foundationally prepare me for a life-altering experience. My obedience, my submission of what I wanted, was part of the essential preparation I would need for the storm brewing just around the corner. It was the beginning of learning to be still.

The next nine months were an absolute whirlwind. The first day of my course, I looked around the room, taking in the other participants. I tried to hide my nerves by arranging my supplies. I fumbled over words to introduce myself. I felt like such an imposter. The content demanded so much time and energy that I wondered how I would ever get through it. As the days progressed, I was surprised to find I enjoyed everything I was learning. I was being challenged, and stretched, but also began to experience confirmation I was on the right path. At the end of each portion of the preparation process, I would pat myself on the back. *There, Heather, good for you, you took the next step. That's all God wanted, just to teach you some obedience. Now you're done.* But at each junction, God made it clear I was to keep going. I kept telling him I didn't understand what he was doing, but I kept taking the next step. It was like putting one foot in front of the other when you don't have any idea where all of those footsteps will take you. I wasn't pursuing anything other than obedience to God.

In the fall, as I was completing the final massive practicum assignment, the competition opened for being a vice principal. This is a huge undertaking. Beyond résumé preparation, the process involved professional philosophy statements, portfolio reviews, case studies, multiple interviews, and a formal presentation. Many people who are incredibly motivated go through this process and are not successful. It's not unusual for people to take two or three times to be successful. I thought maybe I would apply the following spring. After all, I was still writing my practicum, which was substantial, and I needed to have it submitted before taking the next step. Again, God made it clear to me I was to go ahead and apply. My practicum supervisor felt satisfied with the writing and quickly gave me the green light, removing the last barrier. It was daunting to think about. The competition had six different rounds, and people were eliminated along the way. I remember thinking at each round there wasn't any way I would be successful, and then I would make it through. I laughed many times and spoke right out loud, "God what in the world are you doing? I only agreed to the next step." In December I received a phone call congratulating me on being successful. I could hardly make sense of the words. God had taken me on a whirlwind journey, to a place I didn't seek, to do a job I never thought I would do.

God got my attention, focused my efforts, and taught me obedience without knowing the outcome, only the next step. I was full of doubts along the way. I sat through many classes feeling like an imposter. I didn't even tell anyone at work what I was doing because I feared their reaction. Who was I to think I could lead people? During those days of doubting, I had a conversation with a colleague. It was the end of the day in a quiet building, and we were sharing how our days had gone. There was nothing profound, just a friendly chat without children around.

At the end of the conversation, she looked straight at me and said, "I just want you to know, I would totally work for you." Then she said goodnight and walked away. I was stunned. She didn't even know what I was up to. God knew I had serious doubts, and he prompted her to share her thoughts. Over and over again, God spoke to me, affirmed his direction, and reassured me I was on the right path. It was like he started walking closer, being just within arm's reach when I needed him. My confidence grew, but it wasn't confidence in myself. It was a confidence God really was who he says he is, he is really in charge, and he will never leave me. I began to know he is God in a deeper, personal way. The process built a new anchor for my faith. Little did I know that anchor was about to be deeply tested. A massive storm was brewing just around the corner.

Chapter 1

Be still and know that I am God.
Psalm 46:10 NIV

Bright, fluorescent lights flash by overhead. Foreign sounds come from all angles, voices fade in and out, stretcher wheels hum on the floor. The movement down the hall causes confusion, fear, and dread. I shouldn't be here.

The year 2020 is burned into our minds. It's a collective marker in history we each experienced individually, and yet it was an extraordinary shared experience. I started that year in a brand-new job, at a new school, with all new people. My emotions cartwheeled around excitement, nervousness, anticipation, fear, and apprehension. Despite all those emotions, I experienced peace. I knew I was where God alone had placed me. The journey that led to the job taught me I must obey God's direction, and he will be faithful to give it when I seek him. My faith was firm that God would be enough for this new experience.

I dove into learning the job and spent the next three months on an intense learning curve. I sought his guidance continually, having conversations with Jesus as I walked the halls to the next crisis. By March, I found myself extra tired. Our spring break approached, and I was really looking forward to a week off, the rest it would give me. It was a little surreal to reflect that it had only been a year since God had changed the direction of my work. It felt like he put me on a path and then kept whispering, "Hurry up. You need to keep going." There had been an urgency to the whole process.

In my part of the world, the pandemic showed up in March. Just before the scheduled break, it was announced the schools would not reopen to in-person learning. Staff were directed to take all personal belongings home, take everything you would need for teaching from home, and don't leave anything live, such as plants, in the rooms. It was unreal. It felt ominous. What was happening? What did the future hold?

That week, I slept a lot. I started experiencing fatigue like nothing else. When I was awake, all I could think about was when I could go back to sleep. I would sleep for hours and wake up exhausted. It didn't make sense. I should be catching up, regaining my energy. I knew I had been working hard, and I figured the stress of the new job must have been more than I realized.

We started back to school virtually. That was a whole learning experience. Every day involved solving new challenges we had never faced before. I discovered sitting the whole day in front of a screen was not a pleasant experience. I felt more tired than ever. I blamed it on the virtual environment.

Then one day, I noticed my right leg felt kind of funny, sort of weak. It wouldn't work properly when I went up and down the stairs. I gripped the railing to make sure I didn't fall. This weakness progressed over a couple of days, and soon I needed to hold the wall just to walk.

The fatigue piled on and felt like a weight pressing down on all sides. I made an appointment to see the doctor. They initially offered a virtual appointment because of the pandemic, but when the doctor heard my symptoms, she wanted to see me in person. Keith drove me to the appointment, because by that point I couldn't walk without assistance and driving was out of the question.

At the appointment the doctor examined me, didn't say a whole lot, printed off my medical chart and handed it to me. "You need to go to the hospital, and you need to go straight there from here."

Oh, good grief. This doctor is overreacting! I was having a hard time comprehending what she said. I had to get home so I could get back to work. Why didn't she tell me what was wrong with my leg? I remember leaving the doctor's office wondering what was going on. I wasn't worried but puzzled.

We called our three sons from the road, letting them know where we were headed. All I could tell them was I had weakness in my right leg and the doctor sent me to the hospital. There was no sense in them coming to the hospital as they wouldn't be allowed in anyway. Thanks to Covid, there were very tight restrictions.

When we arrived, Keith had to get a wheelchair to get me into the hospital. It was almost dreamlike. I had a hard time comprehending everything that was happening. As they were registering me, the woman looked at me, then at Keith. "You can wheel her down the hall yourself." We had no idea how important that decision would be for us. Once I entered the emergency room area, things started to happen quickly. Keith was told he could stay with me but couldn't leave the curtained area where I was. An intern examined me first and then a doctor. They started an IV and sent me for a scan. I began to wonder if this might be a little more serious than I thought. Back from the scan, Keith and I prayed together, and I thanked God for arranging for Keith to be with me.

My experience with hospital ERs is one of waiting, often for long periods. This time was totally different. Within two hours of entering the hospital, two doctors stood in front of us. They both lowered their masks, and their faces were very serious. *What is happening? They look so serious. This can't be good!* They informed us that I had a brain tumor. Shock rolled through like a bulldozer, taking out everything that was standing in its path.

This must be a mistake. I've always been healthy, rarely sick, and I work in classrooms that can be like petri dishes. A brain tumor! I looked at Keith. His face mirrored the shock, confusion, and pain I felt. How was this happening to us? Why was this happening to us? The doctors explained that I would be admitted for further imaging. Thanks to the Covid protocols, this would mean saying goodbye to Keith. I had just been given the worst news of my life, and now they were going to separate me from my husband. I would have to stay at the hospital, separated from everyone I loved, and try to process the news that I had a brain tumor by myself. This was too much. My mind swirled. *I can't do this! I don't want to do this! Someone tell me it's a mistake!*

I was wheeled up to the neurology floor and taken to a room. It was evening by then and there wasn't a lot of activity. I looked around at my surroundings but didn't really take anything in. It was like my mind couldn't make the proper connections; the thoughts just wouldn't connect. My entire body was reeling, waves of disbelief and shock washed over me relentlessly.

Questions pounded in my head. *What? Brain tumor—this is bad! How did this happen? Why is this happening? What does this mean? Will I ever walk again?* At some point I broke. It was like a dam let loose and the grief and pain came rushing over, flooding every fiber of my being. I sobbed like never before. Those tears were fuelled by fear, by grief, by uncertainty, by anger, by loneliness. Even now as I write this, the pain of that moment rises up and I experience the intensity of it again. I remember thinking I just wanted to scream but didn't want to have nurses come rushing and disturb everyone else. So, I sobbed as quietly as I could.

I'm not sure how long I cried. I was completely disconnected with time. At one point, the nurses came in to give meds to the others in the room. The nurse who checked on me had compassionate eyes above her mask. She took in my tear-stained face. When she asked if I needed anything, I could hardly comprehend the question. I had started my day in the comfortable familiarity of my own bed, and now I didn't recognize anything. "You've had quite a night. Try to get some sleep." I could hear the kindness in her voice, but it didn't really connect. How was I supposed to sleep?

As the night marched on, my tears eventually ran dry. I felt hollowed out, empty, and exhausted. The reality of my circumstances was creeping into my being and slowly demanding to be acknowledged. I had a brain tumor. My life was completely upside down. I had absolutely no control. When met with challenges I was used to taking action. Now my default mode of "doing" was useless. I was stuck in a hospital bed, alone, and scared. As the quiet of the night overtook my room I noticed the sounds around me, the rustle of my roommates, the footfalls in the hallway, the beeps of all the monitors. In that quiet I began to pray.

Up to that point my prayers had been single words. "What? Why? Help!" Now I was able to focus my mind and my heart more. I found myself experiencing a stillness unknown to me. I was stuck in this time and place, with no control over what was happening to me. It was a forced stillness, new and uncomfortable. I didn't want to be here. I was desperate for someone to wake me up from the nightmare. Yet the stillness provided space for my mind to quiet down a bit, for the speed of my racing thoughts to slow down from their frantic pace.

In that stillness, I was able to put words to my thoughts and turn my full attention to God. As I poured out my heart to God, I knew with utmost certainty that he was right there with me, listening to every word. It was raw, honest prayer. I had been stripped down to the end of myself and knew Jesus was the only thing I had. It took every ounce of strength just to form the words. My prayers expressed the agony of the experience. *Oh God please no, no, no! Why is this happening? God, please make this stop! How did this happen? Please help me! I can't do this, God! Please help my family! Jesus, I'm scared!* I had never gone to that depth of pleading before.

Life has a way of handing us circumstances that challenge our faith. This was one of those times for me. I was presented with a choice there on the hospital bed, my pillow soaked with my grief. Did I really believe God was enough for these circumstances? Was he really God, and if he was, what did that really mean? I was still, but did I know he was God? You see, the thing about this verse is there is a period there. Be still and know that I am God, *period.*

There's nothing else asked of us. I must stake everything on the belief that God is who he says he is. It strips away all of the fringe things that can become part of our faith and exposes the core of our belief. Lying in that hospital bed, in the middle of a long, dark night, I was forced to confront the core of my faith. There was a choice to be made. I had been a follower of Jesus for a long time, but did I really believe God is who he says he is? Was I willing to be still and know he is God?

What does it mean to know something? The thirst to know things has driven humanity since the beginning. It has led to all kinds of discoveries and taken the human race beyond the borders of our planet. It has also been the driving force behind the development and success of things like social media.

This desire to know can challenge us to grow, but it can also take us to places leading to destruction. After all, the human drive to know was behind the temptation and ultimately the sin by Adam and Eve.[1] They had the privilege of knowing God intimately, communing daily with the physical presence of the Almighty. They knew God in such a personal way, who met their every need. Yet they wanted to know what God knows, to understand all knowledge. They were tempted with the desire to be like God. The relationship they had with God wasn't enough.

It wasn't just about knowing God and all the intimacy they shared with him in the garden. The temptation to be like God proved overwhelming. In essence, giving in to this temptation signaled that their circumstances were not enough. They had a personal, intimate relationship with the creator, but somehow that wasn't enough. They wanted to be like God, to possess divine knowledge.

Seems a little ungrateful at first glance. Here they are living in perfection, with everything in creation providing their needs. Almighty God is a daily real presence in their lives. Seems like perfection. Why want more?

I'd like to think I would have sent that serpent packing straight away. I would have seen through his deceit and the lies he spewed. I would have run to God and told on the nasty snake! But that's just arrogant thinking. Adam and Eve knew God in ways I am only scratching the surface of. The reality of having a relationship with God is we will be confronted with our limits and get to the end of ourselves pretty quickly.

He commanded us to be still and know he is God. The distinction between who he is and who we are is clear. Blurring that line leads to all kinds of difficulty. You only have to continue reading the story to see that Adam and Eve faced a whole new reality once they disrespected the boundaries, one including pain and suffering.

Having the comfort of my health suddenly stripped away forced me to consider what I really believed about God. It was like running up against a cement wall. No matter where I looked, I couldn't see a way around it. There wasn't anywhere to go, and I was forced to confront my beliefs. Did I really believe God is real? Was he really the almighty, powerful creator? Lying in a hospital room wracked with grief, pain, and uncertainty, was he enough for this circumstance?

You see, in the garden, God was enough for Adam and Eve, until they made the decision he wasn't. God didn't change who he was; their perspective changed. Now at this crossroad in my life, I faced a challenge to the foundation of my faith. What perspective was I going to choose? In walking with God, did I really know He was God without any doubt?

Foundations are one of those things I don't really give much thought. I walk into all kinds of buildings and notice the aesthetics but never consider what makes the building possible. Without the foundation, purposefully laid, nothing lasting is built. There are different materials used to build on, from wooden platforms to poured cement. Some are more lasting than others. If I want my life to truly be built on God, then I have to be purposeful about a lasting foundation.

As I wrestled with my questions, God brought to my mind the whole previous year's journey, the process he took me through to prepare for a new direction at work. He deliberately took me on a journey, down a path that I didn't choose. I never felt alone in that process. I couldn't see the end, but I was confident of the direction. God gave me exactly what I needed when I needed it. I knew in my heart he was my God, and he was in charge.

So, I took what God had carefully built and applied it to my new circumstances. God had been building the foundation of my faith through those experiences, and now I had to rely on that foundation. I chose to believe God was still with me, he knew the path I was on, and he would give me exactly what I needed when I needed it. It was a real act of my will to decide that I was going to believe he is God.

At some point in the middle of that night, the same kind nurse showed up at my bedside again. "Still not able to sleep?" I could only shake my head no. "That's un-derstandable." She paused thoughtfully, then continued. "Your body really does need sleep though. Why don't I get you something to help you sleep?"

I shrugged and managed to croak out "Okay." She brought me a pill and a blanket and helped me arrange myself more comfortably. As I laid there, waiting for the magic of that medication to kick in, I continued to talk to God. *Okay, Lord, I've decided. I believe you are God. Please help me!*

God, I will be still and know that you are God.

Chapter 2

God is our refuge and strength,
an ever-present help in trouble.
Therefore we will not fear.
Psalm 46:1–2a, NIV

Hospitals. What's your gut reaction to them? Many hate them, dread being inside of one. I have not spent a lot of time in hospitals. I had my appendix taken out when I was thirteen, delivered each of our three sons at a hospital, and since then I'd only been a visitor. Now I was stuck inside of a hospital, not knowing when I would ever leave ... if I would ever leave.

I've stood at people's hospital bedsides and struggled to find words. During our time in pastoral ministry I would sometimes go with my husband on a hospital visit to a congregant. I was always amazed at the ease of the conversation, the caring he was able to communicate. During my stay in the hospital, Covid protocols did not allow any visitors, and I was desperate for conversation. The hospital staff was extremely busy, so there was no chance for casual conversations there.

When the chaplain came by my room, I welcomed the opportunity to talk with someone. I had seen God work through the visits Keith had. I knew the opportunity to have a meaningful conversation had presented itself, and I didn't want to miss the opening. The nice thing about having hospital staff talk to you is you don't have to explain everything about your situation.

The chaplain had read my file and knew the seriousness of my illness. She made some gentle inquiries about how I was adjusting to hospital life and gradually worked around to asking how I was handling everything. I wasn't sure how to answer because I didn't think I was handling anything. I was living hour by hour, navigating the uncertainty with unsteady feet. Shock and fear had taken up residence in my mind, and it seemed I was in this vortex of waiting. I could only think of one thing to say. "I'm spending a lot of time praying and reading my Bible. That's all I've got."

Her response surprised me. "That's wonderful." Why would she think that was wonderful? What other option did I have? Didn't she get what I was going through? I was alone, and unable to even use the bathroom without assistance. I had a brain tumor growing in me that doctors were trying to figure out what to do with. There was no relief in sight, just a giant wall of uncertainty.

She offered to pray for me, and I accepted. As she prayed, she thanked God he was with me, that he offers strength, and he is a source of comfort. She also thanked God that I was trusting in him and reading his Word. As she left, I mulled over her words. Was I really trusting God? Sure, I was reading my Bible, but what else was I supposed to do? The days were long, and I had to fill them somehow. I didn't see anything really wonderful about it.

Dawn to dusk passed repeatedly, and I was losing track of the days. Medication slowly reduced the swelling in my brain, to the point where I could plod along with a walker. Soon I was able to support myself completely. I roamed the halls of my ward, doing endless laps just for something to do. It was a depressing place. You didn't land on the neurology ward unless things were very serious. I was grateful for my ability to walk, to talk, to have my mind functioning. I looked like I didn't belong there.

The testing and scans continued. They decided to operate and remove the tumor. I was excited and relieved there was a course of action. The doer in me rejoiced that something would happen. The difficulty came in the timing. Covid had changed everything in the hospital, and only the most serious of surgeries were being performed. Staff were deployed from their usual positions in order to meet the crushing weight of all those desperately sick with Covid.

When I met with the surgeon, he explained the challenge of gathering the team he needed. He only wanted certain people for the different positions, and it would take a bit of time to arrange everyone's schedule. I trusted his decision. He was the top neurosurgeon at the hospital. A nurse friend of mine found out his name and had inquired about him. Turns out he taught other surgeons all around the country the procedure he would perform on me. This was deeply reassuring.

Every couple of days someone would stop by to update me. My hopes would surge and then dash with the words, "No surgery date scheduled yet." A week passed, then ten days. I fell into a routine of reading, doing laps several times a day, and video chatting with family and friends. I learned the best food to order. A friend sent a care package full of wonderful treats. That became my daily highlight, to indulge in "real" food.

Never before did I have so much time on my hands. The doer in me became easily frustrated. The days were so long. My mind was my worst enemy. That much time allowed so many thoughts to churn. I could feel the anxiety rising, building up, and I didn't like how that felt. I began to search Scripture to find answers to all the questions and uncertainty that reigned. After all, I finally had plenty of time to read my Bible.

The story of Joseph was familiar to me, and yet when I read it in the hospital, I was riveted. In Genesis 37, Joseph's story starts with tension and strife woven into the family relationships. Joseph "tattled" on his half-brothers, giving his father, Israel, bad reports about them. Israel favored Joseph, stoking the tension into hatred.

Then Joseph had dreams, and in youthful enthusiasm, shared them with his family. This got everyone up in arms. Even his father reprimanded Joseph for the audacity of what he spoke. By the time Joseph's brothers revolted and got rid of Joseph by selling him off to slave traders, Joseph had experienced the sting of disbelief and hatred from his entire family.

I can't imagine the confusion, shock, and pain Joseph experienced as he travelled to Egypt. God didn't leave him though, and he prospered in Egypt, gaining recognition in Pharaoh's house. That recognition brought him onto the radar of Potiphar's wife. His refusal to sleep with her led to his prison time.

There was Joseph, rejected by family, having to live in the unfamiliar surroundings of a foreign land, being unjustly punished for doing the right thing. I can hardly begin to envision what Joseph was experiencing in jail. Did he despair? It would be totally understandable. Was he angry? Totally justifiable. Was he tempted to fold into the emotion of it all, and bury himself in all the hurt? Easily done.

Joseph spent huge amounts of time waiting, sitting in pits of uncertainty. What really struck me was his hope in God remained intact. Ultimately, God fulfilled a purpose so much bigger than what Joseph could see. The timing of that purpose though, played out over years. How did He ever survive?

If God could faithfully bring Joseph through all of that, could he bring me through too? The question stared me in the face. I was being tempted to give into despair that wouldn't leave. I knew I needed to allow God to work in my heart and mind to bring me to a place of peace. I read more, spending longer periods of time reading whole sections of Scripture.

In my prayers, I poured out my fears to God, begging for something to get me through. What I really needed was more of God, and as this slowly dawned on me, my prayers got bolder. This was bigger than my resources. I needed God to intercede and calm my mind and my spirit.

One day I was reading in the Psalms and came across these words, "God is our refuge and strength, an ever-present help in trouble. Therefore, we will not fear." (Psalm 46:1–2a, NIV)

The present tense of the verse landed in my being with a thud. The psalmist was not saying God would help at some point when he got around to it. The help is "ever-present", always there and current to every situation.

God offered me help in every minute of those long days. I could go to him and he promised to be a refuge when the uncertainty and fear overtook my mind. The idea of refuge was so appealing. I was in a room with three other people and a constant flow of nurses and doctors. I had nowhere to be by myself, to take refuge from the barrage of events dictating my life. But God promised he would be a place where I could get away, find rest, and be safe. I decided to take God at His word, and I prayed those words over and over.

One of my biggest worries during that time was for my family. I knew this was turning their worlds upside down too. The stress and fear were not isolated to me, it was a family experience. I talked to Keith and each of our sons every day. It was a lifeline to me, but also a way for them to walk through the uncertainty. In those daily video chats, I could see the worry lines on their faces. It wasn't verbalized too much. I'm used to that. In a house full of males, the expression of emotion is not a regular thing, unless it's over a sporting event.

The certainty of their lives was uprooted, and I hated it. It felt so unfair. Our sons were just getting their lives going, launching as adults. Keith had recently retired from ministry and was finding a new rhythm in his renovation work. These men were my world and should not be forced to face the uncertainty of whether I was going to live or not.

To top it all off, I couldn't be with them, hug them, reassure them with my presence. We needed to be to-gether physically and gain the strength that comes from being with those you love most. I wondered how they were dealing with everything. Brave faces always smiled at me through the camera, but what was happening when the screen turned off?

Several times each day, I would find myself praying for them. Actually, it would be more appropriately described as begging God to take care of them. The mom in me had lost the ability to care for my family like I always had. I knew each of them so well and knew what I would do if I was with them. It was painful to not be able to take care of them how I wanted to.

One of the downsides of the medication was sleeplessness. I would lie awake for hours on end, trying to sleep. Often, I would get a few hours, then wake up like it was morning, even though it was only 2:00 a.m. During those times, I spent a lot of time praying. Talking to Jesus was a way to slow down my swirling mind, bringing order to my thoughts. In honesty, I admitted my fears to God, one of the biggest being a fear for my family. I exposed the ache in my heart for them to Jesus. I pleaded for them to be okay. I couldn't always find words to express myself, but the ache in my heart cried out.

One morning, after yet another night of pleading with God for my family, I turned to my Bible and read Isaiah 43. "When you walk through the fire, you will not be burned; the flames will not set you ablaze." (Isaiah 43:2b, NIV) I had read this chapter many times, yet that morning as I meditated on what God's words meant for me, the weight of the burden I carried for my family pressed in from all sides.

So, I did the only thing I could do and laid the burden at Jesus' feet. In that desperate place, God spoke to me. It was quite powerful, almost like an audible voice, declaring the promise of that verse. "When you walk through the fire, you will not be burned; the flames will not set you ablaze." (Isaiah 43:2b, NIV)

Then I saw Keith and our three sons going through a fire, but they were above it. The flames were reaching up towards them, but they were safe above. Flames were not consuming or harming them. I looked down and there was Jesus, holding all four of them. He was walking, carrying my family through the fire. It wasn't a frantic or fearful pace, just a bold, confident walk. I heard Jesus telling me, "I've got them, Heather. I've got your family. I've got them."

I sat there for a long time after the vision ended. I had never experienced anything like that before. The power of what I saw and heard was magnificent. It wasn't like waking up from sleeping. I knew I wasn't dreaming because I was sitting up and it was the middle of the morning. I looked around and the room looked the same. My roommates were going about their morning routines, staff coming and going as usual.

But I was different. The burdensome weight I had felt for my family was gone. In its place I felt a confidence and peace. Oh, that peace was such a welcome arrival! I had experienced the power of almighty God, felt his strength. I was overwhelmed with the depth of God's love. I knew with complete certainty God was in total control. He didn't miss anything. He knew the depth of my pain for my family, and he was working in ways I didn't know about. Isaiah 43 talks about God making a way through hard things. I realized God was making a way for my family and I to get through the storm. This brought reassurance and peace, leaving me awestruck by his kindness and care.

This was a pivotal moment. It changed me, and my approach to the time of waiting I was in. I operated from a different perspective, one that was driven by peace and confidence in God. Things started to look different. I saw my roommates through fresh eyes. Each one was in their own crisis point, and I began to recognize the fear and uncertainty in their eyes. I started to engage them in conversations, asking about their lives, their loved ones. I determined I would try to demonstrate kindness to each one and bless them with some encouragement. This was something out of my comfort zone, but I couldn't just sit on the gift God had given me. I had peace and I needed to share it.

In the quiet conversations, eventually our medical situations came up. There weren't a whole lot of secrets in a room divided only by curtains. We each had an idea of what the others were facing. The question of "How are you doing today?" was loaded but also gave an opportunity to share when there was such limited chance to do so. Often the best thing to do was listen. I had lots of time and decided giving some of it to my roommates would be what Jesus would want me to do.

Eventually questions would boomerang back to me. They all knew I was waiting for a craniotomy to remove a tumor. One day a roommate remarked they didn't know how I was handling things so well. I explained I spend a lot of time reading my Bible and praying, and God was the one getting me through. She nodded an acknowledgement. There wasn't much more said but I knew everyone was watching. They had seen me reading and praying. I kept trying to be an encouragement each day. God was with me in that room, and I did my best to share his love and kindness.

In looking to minister to others, there was a sense of purpose. The "doer" in me connected with that, but more than that, I felt like I was not just surviving anymore. The days seemed to go by a little quicker. I wasn't feeling so weighed down. My confidence in God gave me space to approach each day with the expectation God was working. Some of those I video chatted with remarked they didn't know how I was doing it, how I was so calm. Again, I pointed out that any calmness they could see was God at work.

This peace was challenged when I got my surgery date. I was excited to get the news. Finally, they were going to do something. My surgeon met with me to explain the procedure. They would be performing an awake craniotomy. He went over things in great detail. I was struck with the magnitude of what they would be doing. He described things I had seen on television shows or movies, but never considered would be my reality.

I tried hard to focus on his words, but I could feel anxiety rising. His manner was confident, and I appreciated that he didn't rush through things, took time to answer my questions, and reassured me that everyone involved was specifically chosen by him for their excellence. When I got back to my room, I spent the next little while sharing the news. The wait had been long for everyone.

Once I had shared the news with everyone, I settled into another evening of reading. As I tried to focus on the words on the page, other words leapt into my mind. *Awake craniotomy, tumor resection, skull removal, brain mapping.* This was major surgery. The risks were real. I was really going to have my brain operated on. My stomach began to churn, and I could feel my breathing change. The more I thought about what they were going to do to me, the more the doubt rose. *I can't do this. So many things could go wrong. Why is this happening? I don't want this to be my reality.*

As the thoughts galloped through my mind, I struggled to rein them in. They were too strong for me though, like a horse who has been spooked and will not slow down no matter what the rider does. Full-blown panic was just around the corner, and desperation would drive me there. I grabbed my Bible and searched for some calm. "You are my refuge and strength, an ever-present help in trouble. Therefore, I will not fear." Over and over, I spoke that verse, personalizing it, whispering the words to myself to make them more real.

I went back to Isaiah 43. I read and reread how God is with us when we are going through deep waters. I claimed the promise the waters of fear would not sweep over me. *Is God enough for an awake craniotomy?* He had proved himself enough so far in this storm, so I chose to believe He would be enough for this surgery. Again, it was a choice to place myself completely in His control. This went against my natural instincts, and I had to recite Scripture over and over as a weapon against fear.

I was so frustrated. Inadequacy coupled with the fear to create a toxic mix that led to defeat. After all, the verse says, "We will not fear." Guess I just wasn't strong enough for this. I couldn't do it. But that was the whole point! I wasn't strong enough for this, but I didn't have to be. God could do it. He was strong enough. He knew fear would show up and gave me his words and then brought them to my mind. They were the weapons I needed for this battle, because the battle was really God's.

Fear not. It's a command, but not some harsh unrealistic expectation. When God commands us not to fear, he places his promises right alongside the command. Our circumstances can look bleak. Oftentimes the thing we face seems insurmountable. The relationship is unsalvageable, the financial hole is too deep, the health issue leaves us wasted, the depression is too dark. Examined from all human angles, the challenge is just too great. The fear is completely justified. After all, we have done everything possible and found no solution. Nothing is going to change, and we are in danger of being carried under by the weight of the fear.

When we're pulled under a wave of fear, panic sets in. I was in Mexico as a teenager, enjoying a day of fun on the beach. Long, thick ropes were anchored high on the beach and led out into the water. You couldn't see where they ended. As we walked along, playing in the waves, I was distracted by my friends. I didn't notice the huge wave coming in. Suddenly, I was kicked off my feet and could feel the undertow of a wave pulling me down and out.

I had been caught completely off guard, and I desperately fought to get to the surface. As I struggled, my hand caught something, and I latched on. It was one of those ropes. I hung on with all my might, and as the power of the wave passed, I was able to pull myself along the rope, getting to the surface and the air I was desperate for.

Life can be like those waves. We often get knocked down. We don't see what is coming, and suddenly we are in a desperate situation. God's Word is like those ropes. He anchors his promises among the waves, knowing when and where they will be needed. His provision is already there when we are knocked off our feet.

Joseph experienced the power of those waves. He didn't see the betrayal of his brothers coming, didn't expect to be thrown in prison for refusing to have an affair.

The circumstances the people of Israel were facing in Isaiah 43 seemed insurmountable. The army of Babylon was powerful, proven to be conquerors. The strong wave of this army was cresting, threatening to wash the Israelites away. God responded to this threat by speaking something even more powerful than the might of the Babylonian army. "Fear not, for I have redeemed you; I have called you by name, you are mine." (Isaiah 43:1b, ESV) This is God's answer to our fears, knowing we are his.

He will hold us close when the waves wash over. He will care for us, protect us, and lead us to the air. God was there for Joseph in the pit of prison, he was there for the people of Israel facing odds stacked against them. He is our creator and redeemer, and that is a very personal level of ownership. The kind of ownership that brings peace because God is intimately involved in all the details of our lives. The pairing of this command and promise is a strong, thick rope, available for us to grab and hang on to.

The day before my surgery arrived. Anticipation woke me up, but it was free of the dread previously dominating my thoughts. I spent the day connecting with family and friends. I worked on writing some notes to my sons and Keith. I knew I was arranging loose ends, communicating with people meaningfully, measuring my words carefully. Yes, the thoughts were there. *I may not be able to communicate after this. I might not even make it through this.* It wasn't causing me fear or panic though, just a strong determination to ensure that everyone I cared about knew how much I loved them.

That night, I remember thinking there was no way I was going to be able to sleep. So, I was shocked when someone woke me up. It was daylight, and they were telling me it was time to get ready to go. There wasn't much to do. I had arranged everything the night before. I sat on the edge of the bed, bowed my head, and talked to Jesus. I affirmed my belief in him, my trust in him, and claimed those promises that he would be with me. I remember thinking as I laid in the hallway outside the operating room that I should be scared. Try as I might, I just couldn't find any fear, only an amazing sense of peace. *You're right here, aren't you God. This is not me God; it's all you. Your peace is covering me completely. Stay right here, Lord.* It was all God! He was enough.

God, I will be still and know that you are God.

You are my refuge and strength, an ever-present help in trouble. Therefore, I will not fear.

Chapter 3

As for me, I will always have hope;
I will praise you more and more.
Psalm 71:14, NIV

Hope is a funny thing. It's intangible, and yet so very real. It can carry someone through horrible circumstances but then vanish in an instant. The dictionary defines it as "a feeling of expectation and a desire for a certain thing to happen."[2] When I became conscious after my craniotomy, I had a singular hope: that the tumor was totally gone.

If I'm completely honest, I also hoped that I would still have all my cognitive and motor abilities intact. I had specific outcomes I was hoping for. While the fog of anesthetic slowly lifted, I threw up prayers of hope for good news. They were small snippets of thought as my mind began to make sense of what my body had just been through. *Hey, I'm still alive. I can move my body. I can even speak.*

I drifted in and out more times than I could count. Each time I woke, I took inventory of what I felt and how my body was responding. At some point, I woke to the surgeon beside me. He confidently spoke the words I had been hoping to hear. "You did great. I was able to remove the whole tumor."

With surgery over, the whole focus of my existence in the hospital changed. No longer was it about waiting. Now it was about getting out of there. The staff had me up on my feet and moving around very quickly. Those initial, shaky steps soon turned into unassisted tours around the room. The focus required to make my body move decreased and the strength built.

The final hurdle to overcome was stairs. I had to be able to navigate stairs to be released. I looked forward to the physiotherapy appointments. It was tiring, but I was desperate to see my family again, so I pushed through. Within a few days the doctor came with those precious words, "You can go home today." It was what I had hoped for, and the praise rolled off my lips.

It's hard to find the right words to describe how it felt to see my family again. We often have times where we are separated from family. Sometimes it's a choice, like taking a trip or going to study in a different city. Employment can take us to new locations, away from our loved ones. Friends move away, making those chances for a coffee together vanish. Covid forced separation on us in new and uncomfortable ways. Being apart physically from those we love is hard.

When I saw my family again in person, I was over-whelmed with a barrage of emotions. Relief led the parade. I had wondered if I would ever be with my family again, and now I could touch them. My heart was bursting with joy at their presence. As I studied those wonderful faces, I discovered new lines that the stress of my illness had etched into their countenances. I could see the concern and worry still prominent, even under the happy smiles. I was struck with sadness for what they had been forced into experiencing.

It was a mix of opposites, experiencing immense joy and heartbreaking sadness at the same time. Isn't that what life is so often? It's both so incredibly wonderful, and so incredibly painful. Life in all its fullness does not mean one or the other is left out. This was the beginning of a new learning curve for me.

Recuperation was an unfamiliar experience for Keith and I. Sure there had been times when one of us was sick, and we stepped up to care for the other, but these were relatively minor and short-lived times. As a mom, I had nursed the boys through a whole variety of childhood illnesses and injuries.

Now, I was forced to be dependent on others in a way that felt very foreign to me. While I could walk, I needed assistance as my balance was very unsteady. When I wanted something, someone got it for me. When I needed to go somewhere, an extra set of hands was required. At first, I felt like an imposition. I was the caregiver in the family and now the roles were reversed. It's funny how we define ourselves, whether we realize it or not. The perspective we have on our self-worth can get so wrapped up and distorted. I had willingly cared for my family for years, and now that I needed them to care for me, I was uncomfortable. We had to learn a new rhythm for this new season.

After being home for a couple of weeks, I had an appointment with an oncologist. I wasn't sure what this would hold. Just being connected with an oncologist raises anxiety. I didn't spend a lot of time thinking about it though, because I was consumed with the physical task of healing from the craniotomy. When the body makes those kinds of demands, there isn't a lot of room mentally to consider or think about other things. Thanks to Covid, I would have to do this appointment by myself. My big focus as I walked into the hospital was being able to navigate the walk down the halls. I had no idea how far I would have to go, and I didn't want to run out of strength before I reached my destination. *God, please get me there!* When I arrived at the room, I was relieved.

The oncologist appeared and began to review my case with me. I had Keith dialed in from the parking lot, and I tried to focus on taking notes so I could figure out how to make sense of all the information.

While I was in the hospital, they had performed a biopsy on a preexisting lump in my armpit. This was something I had discovered a few months before. I had already previously undergone an ultrasound and a biopsy, and these results came back as benign. Now, as the oncologist began to speak, I could hear the seriousness in her tone. It was hard to read her face from behind the mask, but her eyes were serious and a little sympathetic.

The results from both the brain and the armpit areas confirmed cancer. *Oh wow!* Stage 4, metastatic melanoma. *What, this can't be happening!* The original site was the armpit, and it had then spread to my brain. *Keith, I need you beside me!* At some point I think my listening failed, and I was overcome with an unfamiliar pain. It was a strange mix of shock, grief, anger, disbelief, and sorrow. *This can't be true!* Then the doctor paused and looked right at me. "This is very serious. You need to go home and get your affairs in order." *What? My affairs? That's what dying people do!*

When I got back to the car, Keith was very quiet. I was too. What exactly do you say to your spouse when the doctor has just told you the clock is now counting down on your life. I could see the raw emotion in his eyes, and it defied words. When we got home, Keith stayed in the car, saying he was going for a drive. I went upstairs to my bedroom. I needed some time by myself to process this news. Process? That's the polite way to say I was melting down.

The words played on a loop in my mind. *Cancer. Stage 4. Metastatic.* I could feel my emotion rolling into giant balls, hurtling down on me, threatening to bury me. The largest ball of all was anger. It started out small, but like a snowball heading down a hill, it grew as it picked up speed. As it slammed into me, all I could feel was anger radiating through every cell. It pushed out all the other emotions and demanded center stage.

I started to talk to God. Actually, it wasn't really talking, more like an angry rant on high volume. "God what is going on? Why is this happening? I can't have cancer! This isn't fair! Haven't we been through enough, God? We spent twenty-six years in ministry. Didn't we deal with enough? I just started this new job, which was your idea by the way. Why would you lead me to that, just to take it away? The boys are just getting started in life; they shouldn't have to deal with a dying mother! I'm mad, God! So, so mad!" I spoke the words out into the room, kind of yelled them. I just couldn't keep them inside.

I'm not sure how long I spent pacing, ranting to God. Eventually the emotions exhausted me, and I slumped down on the floor. I was a broken mess. My world had fallen completely apart. I was not equipped for this. It was beyond what I could handle. We had been through some extremely stressful circumstances, and I knew I had developed strength from those experiences, but this was completely different. It was out of my control on a whole new level.

Once the anger subsided, I could feel the other big ball of emotion that had been pushing anger down the hill, fear. I was frightened. *God, I need your help! This is beyond me. I don't get it. I don't want it. I can't do it by myself. You have to do this, Jesus. It's gonna have to be your strength 'cause mine isn't there.*

In the book of Job, we find an honest depiction of suffering and the questioning that comes with it. Job questioned God, "Why have you made me your target?" (Job 7:20, NIV) His suffering brought about the questioning that comes to all of us when we are faced with the unthinkable. Why is this happening?

Job doesn't hold back in his own rant to God. "Why didn't I die at birth, my first breath out of the womb my last?" (Job 3:11, MSG) His pain was so great that he wished he had never been born. Job had experienced the loss of his health, his family, his material possessions. His life unraveled, and this left him bewildered and outraged. He had spent his life honouring God, and these losses felt like an unjust punishment. Didn't he deserve to be spared such tremendous, all-consuming agony?

You see, suffering is all around us and we encounter it every day, but when suffering appears unjust, it causes our stomachs to recoil and the anger to rise. As children, we are taught a system of justice; do what you are supposed to do, and things will work out. If you deviate, there are negative consequences. As we get older and experience more of life, we start to run into situations where this simplistic system of justice does not work. Unemployment shows up, violent crimes leave devastated victims, disease overtakes a life, relationships crumble. We can be living our lives, doing our best, and still get blindsided and knocked down.

That was Job's experience, and it is still happening to people today. What do we do with that? How do we respond when we are reeling in pain? I love Job's honest response. He doesn't hold back. He protests, he questions, he gives voice to his pain. Job had spent a lifetime serving God. He had a relationship with the Almighty, and he goes right to the source with his questions. He was doing his best, living his life honouring God and everything was taken from him. I had been doing my best, trying to honour God and follow his guidance, and now my life was being taken from me. Job struggled to make sense of it and so did I. I knew Job's pain and despair, his shock and surprise, his hurt and confusion.

In those hours of agony, I was much like Job. I begged and pleaded with God to stop the nightmare, to take it away. I protested and laid out all the reasons why it shouldn't be happening. I was desperate to just stop it, to wake up and find out it was all a dream. I demanded to know why God would allow such a thing. I went over the initial biopsy misdiagnosis and questioned God's wisdom in not intervening at that point. Nothing was making sense to me anymore, and it felt like I was floating aimlessly on a sea of pain.

Eventually, Keith returned from his drive. I knew he had needed time and space to try and process the horrendous news in his own way. When we looked at each other, we could speak no words. We just held each other for a very long time. I don't think either of us knew what to do, so we did the only thing we could do; we prayed. We asked God to help us. We told him we didn't understand. Then we staked everything we had on God and put our trust in him.

In the following days and weeks, I went back to Job and reread his experience. Over and over, I read his response to the losses. When his entire world fell apart, he did not turn his back on God. "Not once through all this did Job sin, not once did he blame God." (Job 1:22, MSG) His pain was right there, sitting on the surface, but he did not abandon God.

I realized the only way I could continue would be if I stayed with God. It was a decision of the will. It wasn't driven by emotion. I was still angry, confused, and hurt. It would be easy to fall into that abyss of pain and never look up. I knew on my own, that is where I would end up. In my mind's eye I could see a fork in the road. One direction would take me on a path of my own design, the other a direction where God would lead. Neither direction gave a clear picture of what was ahead, just a way of travelling. Did I believe sticking with God would be enough? Would I be able to handle this without him? Did I trust God with my future? When I look back, I know that this was a major crossroad in my journey. I had to decide how I was going to proceed, with or without God.

I didn't understand why God had allowed me to get cancer. I was tempted to shake my fist and turn away. In the depth of my heart, when I was able to quiet the emotion and truly be still, I could hear Jesus' voice. "I love you, Heather. I am still here. You are not alone. I love you." There wasn't an answer to my question of why, but there was this amazing affirmation I was God's child, and he was still with me. He had stayed right with me even in the angry questioning. In fact, he felt closer. The creator of all things, powerful and mighty God was whispering his love to me. I made the decision that I had to continue with God. I had no idea what the coming days would hold. I had no idea what cancer would do to me. I knew my life was full of uncertainty, and in the midst of the realization I knew I desperately needed God. He was the only one who I could give my uncertainty to because I could be certain of his love, and that would be enough.

I spent a lot of time in my Bible during those days. My world had become very small. I was focusing on my recuperation physically, and now trying to cope with the emotional blow of my diagnosis. I would sit with my Bible and ask God to give me something that would help everything make sense. It was hard to connect with people because I was preoccupied. The loop of questions and uncertainty played over and over in my head. When I read my Bible, I had to first quiet all of the emotional noise in my head in order to comprehend and take the words in. It was a struggle a lot of the time, but I kept going. I had to keep going. I had made the decision to stick with God, and now in the steep climb, I didn't want to give up.

I have been a runner, and over the years I've trained for marathons and triathlons. Each time I would prepare for these events, I was struck by the amount of time it takes. There was no shortcut. I learned in order to go the distance you have to increase the training in small amounts. Increase the run too much and you can set yourself back. I understood what it was like to hit the proverbial "wall." There were times in my training where my body and mind went into protest, and together they conspired to get me to stop. I would physically falter, and my mind would tell me I couldn't do it.

During those tough training runs, I learned to give myself short goals. I would tell myself I'd stop at the end of the block, or at the next corner. Then when I got there, I would tell myself "Hey you made it. Let's try for the next block." By taking the long run, and breaking it down into small portions, I changed my focus from the overwhelming task of a long run to the immediate task of completing a short section. Each time I did this, I realized that I actually could keep going and this inspired me to finish the run.

Now I found it was time to use this strategy again, this time in learning to continue with this new direction in my life. Each day I would try to think about just that day, and what I could learn from the Bible that day. I told God I expected to hear from him before I started reading. Slowly the expectation built, and I began to read with fresh eyes.

One day I came upon this verse: "As for me, I will always have hope; I will praise you more and more." (Psalm 71:14, NIV) It was like the verse had a spotlight on it. *Is it possible to always have hope? Where was my hope? What am I hoping for?* I knew I was not full of hope. I needed hope. So, I asked God for hope. It was a simple prayer. The idea of praising God more and more just couldn't happen until he filled me with hope. If God was truly in charge of my life, then I could hope in him. I made this verse my mantra, reciting it several times a day. When the doubt, fear, and anxiety took over, I fought it with this verse. It was a battle, and I used this Scripture as my weapon.

It was a daily process, using God's word against all the fear. It was my way of making it to the end of the block each day. At night I would repeat the verse over and over until I fell asleep. Slowly, just like when I was training for a marathon, I would find that the hope was increasing, the praise was beginning to rise. It was a little more each day. The faithfulness of Scripture to build strength in my life was being realized. I had to do it every day though.

There were times when I would neglect the Scripture, just forge ahead on my own. There wasn't any praise in those days though. I was enduring my life without the hope Jesus brings, and there just wasn't any praise to be found. I learned the importance of daily putting my hope in God through claiming the promises he has given in Scripture. It's not easy; in fact it is grueling, just like my training runs.

The alternative, living in the pain all by myself, was something I knew I couldn't endure, so I asked God to help me keep my focus on him. God was building hope within me, despite my circumstances. I knew it was God's work; there was no way I could do this on my own. In fact, it didn't make sense. How could someone be hopeful with stage 4 cancer? On my own I couldn't, but with Jesus walking with me, there was hope. I was learning God is enough.

God, I will be still and know that you are God.

You are my refuge and strength, an ever-present help in trouble. Therefore, I will not fear.

But as for me, I will always have hope; I will praise you more and more.

Chapter 4

I praise you, Lord, for being my guide. Even
in the darkest night, your teachings fill my
mind. I will always look to you, as you stand
beside me and protect me from fear. With all
my heart, I will celebrate, and I can safely rest.
Psalm 16:7–9, CEV

In the days following my diagnosis, it felt as though I couldn't keep up with everything going on medically. Every day I had to contend with a new phone call, a new appointment. Overnight I had five new doctors following me. They recommended radiation, a second surgery for the lump in my armpit, and more, yet-to-be-determined treatment.

I found the experience mentally tiring. My brain was still healing and not yet firing on all cylinders. I forgot anything not written down. Concentration was short and exhausted me. This was frustrating. I had gone from working all day in a job where you juggle multiple demands to struggling to remember which appointment was happening that day. I would ask my husband questions, and I knew from the look on his face it was something he had already answered. Oh, how I hated this. I wanted my brain to work the way it used to, and I feared the surgery had taken abilities from me that would never return.

The process of healing from brain surgery was so foreign and strange. Many days I wondered whose body I was now in. Between that and the trauma of getting such a serious diagnosis, I was quite a mess. When my mind was able to focus enough to truly take in my circumstances, the emotional toll of facing my cancer would wipe out what little energy I had. I was experiencing a dark night, both physically and emotionally.

Covid added a weird twist to my new reality. I had to keep my distance from people. It was early days in the pandemic, and there was so much unknown about the virus. Contact with people posed a significant threat to me. I ached to be with people, to be hugged, to receive the comfort my loved ones were eager to give. It was so heart-wrenching to watch my mom and dad from the porch, as they stood in the driveway talking to me, sending air hugs across the gap. I wanted to be wrapped up in those hugs, soak in the strength and comfort I would find there. Covid robbed me of those opportunities.

Our sons changed their lives to ensure we could have contact. They took time off, adjusted schedules, and limited their contact with people to allow us to keep a safe bubble so we could still be together. My heart ached for them. Not only were they dealing with a seriously ill parent, but they were not able to access friends for support in person. At a time when we all needed the presence of people in our lives, it was taken away.

I felt like my entire world had completely turned upside down. Nothing was familiar, everything felt strange and uncertain. I vacillated between anger at the new circumstances, to despair that life was never going to get better. Cancer is hard, but cancer during Covid is cruel. I reached the point several times where I was ready to just say, "I don't care!" and start hugging people. Keith was always a voice of reason in those moments, and he would hold me as long as I needed, until my anger and despair would retreat. Those feelings never really left though. They would recede and allow me to get through the day, but they lurked in the background, just waiting to pounce.

Emotions. We all have them, but how much do we really understand them? They can drive our behavior, dictate reactions, and often feel like they are controlling us. Why did God create us with emotions? What was the point? These were some of the many questions that circled around and around in my head. According to the American Psychological Association, emotion is defined as "a complex reaction pattern, involving experiential, behavioral and physiological elements."[3]

Complex is an understatement! My emotions were driving my reactions to the point I felt like I didn't have any control. My mind would not relax, wouldn't shut off, and the worst was at night. One of the continued side effects of the medication I was on was sleeplessness. This plagued me in the hospital, but I thought it would improve once I was back in the quiet and peace of my home. Was I ever wrong!

At night, in the quiet of my home, where I should have been peacefully sleeping, I would spend hours awake and restless. I would get up and roam around the house. We had just completed a kitchen renovation, and I stared at everything that was new. I wandered the rooms, noticing things that were out of place. I contemplated cluttered closets or disorganized drawers. My focus only went to what I saw that was wrong, things that I wanted to change or improve. It was a dissatisfaction, very misplaced. You see, there wasn't anything wrong with my house.

My life felt out of control, and I was desperate to gain some kind of control. So, focusing on physical things I could change or improve became a way to distract myself from the pain of facing my circumstances. Each day I would plan to tackle some job around the house. Then I would try to complete it, only to become physically exhausted and unable. In those moments I became so frustrated. I would cry and let the anger take over.

It took many repetitions of this cycle to realize that my anger had nothing to do with the house. I was angry I had cancer. When I prayed and read my Bible, I would find some peace, but it was momentary, temporary. The anger was never gone. It was like my physical pain. I could take a pill and get relief for a while, but it didn't last. My frustration over this cycle sent me into despair. Why couldn't I get rid of the anger? What did that say about my relationship with Jesus? He had spoken to me and been so close in the hospital. Why had that changed?

I returned to the story of Job in the Bible. Reading it over and over, I felt Job's anger, his despair. It wasn't fair. He had spent his life serving God, trying to be the man God wanted him to be, to honor God with his life. Yet everything was stripped away from him, his suffering and pain immense. At the very beginning of the story, we are told God grants permission for Satan to test Job. That didn't sit well with me. How could a God who is by his very nature loving, allow one of his children to go through suffering. What was the point of it? That question of why screamed at me as I read Job's story.

Job's laments were painful for me to read because they resonated with my own questioning and pain. At the very beginning of his journey, when his physical suffering began, Job made an extraordinary statement. His wife is

encouraging him to curse God. She believes he is justified, after all, she has been a witness to the kind of life
he has lived, and he surely does not deserve this pain.
Job responds with these words: "We take the good days
from God. Why not also the bad days?" (Job 2:10, MSG)

When I read that, the words leapt off the page. I had
been eager to receive the blessings God had poured
out over my life. My marriage to a faithful man, three
healthy sons, work I loved, family and friends who
supported me, all kinds of blessings. Just a couple
years before I was diagnosed, Keith and I celebrated
our twenty-fifth anniversary. We took a trip to Hawaii,
which was a dream come true. I remember describing
it to someone as the trip of a lifetime. Talk about a big
blessing! So here I was, now in a season of suffering.
Could I so easily forget the blessings? Was I prepared
to take the bad days as well as the good? Job's words
cut right through me. At my core I didn't want the
anger to continue. I wanted God to take it. For weeks
I pleaded for this.

The time had come for radiation to begin. Radiation
would involve lying very still on a table, with my head
strapped down under this weird mask, while a long arm
rotated around my head. Hurdle number one was the
mask. At the first appointment, where they explained
everything and made the mold for the mask, I knew I was
facing a hurdle. My claustrophobia kicked in when they

described how the mask would have cutouts for my eyes, but the rest would be a mesh.

The idea of having my head covered in a mask, fastened to a table, sent anxious thoughts exploding through my mind. *I can't do this Lord. No way! You have to help me, God!* As I approached the appointments, I asked people to pray. I got very specific. I was done with general requests. I needed God to work and keep me calm during those appointments. I needed to get this radiation.

Radiation would target the exact areas of my brain that were affected, precise down to the millimeter. I didn't want any lurking cancer cells to remain, and radiation was the way to address that. I just wasn't sure I had the strength to go through it, to remain calm and still. So, I got vulnerable with some people and asked them to pray specifically that I wouldn't feel claustrophobic and would be able to remain calm. I wasn't used to asking for such specific requests, and it felt uncomfortable and strange.

People were very receptive to having something specific to pray for. Every time I walked into an appointment, I knew people were asking God to keep me calm. To say God answered those prayers is an understatement. During those appointments, I found a tremendous sense of peace. Never once did I feel panicked or claustrophobic. On the last one I even drifted off to sleep! God took a very specific request and graciously brought me through.

The radiation brought on a new level of exhaustion to my already tired body. I would start my day with some energy, but at various points the fatigue would just over-whelm me. It was like someone turning out a light switch. I had to sleep immediately. Once I woke, I felt refreshed, right up until the switch got turned off again. I never really knew for sure when I would get tired, so planning to do anything was out of the question.

This slowed me down and forced me to keep a mea-sured pace. I devoted more time to my Bible. Worship music became a peaceful place to spend time in. The fatigue also kept the anger at bay. I was just too tired to be angry. I knew it was still there, simmering on a back burner, but I didn't have the energy to address it.

In the weeks after the radiation finished, my energy levels slowly improved. I still had the switch getting turned off, but it happened less often, and the time in between began to increase. One of the positives of the radiation was that it took away the sleeplessness. Howev-er, as I recovered from the treatments, the sleeplessness slowly returned. The night was once again very long, and my frustration grew. Everything in my life was upended, and I didn't recognize this life I was now in. I hardly recognized myself, both inside and out.

The simmering anger was unsettling. I thought I had dealt with it, but here it was front and center again. I'm not really an angry person, and I hadn't made a practice of keeping angry for long periods of time. One thing that always easily angered me was injustice, and as far as I was concerned, life was not fair right now. As I wandered around the house, I poured out my heart to God, every powerful emotion I was experiencing. The anger came first. It was white hot and fuelled by the question of why. I couldn't reconcile a loving God who would allow this to happen. Getting to the end of the anger was exhausting, but I eventually reached the point where I was all cried out and finished with ranting at God.

There, with no one around to distract me, and my anger spent, God was able to get my attention. He began to bring to my mind other times when I had experienced injustice, or my family had. Reflecting on those situations brought evidence of how God had worked. He had seemed silent in those moments, but looking back, I could see that he was always there, always walking with me. I had a choice to make. What was I going to do with the evidence? Was I going to continue this journey railing against God, pointing out the injustice, blaming him for inactivity?

The alternative would be to embrace the evidence and walk in it. As Jesus gently cleared the emotion away, I realized I was at a critical juncture with a choice to make. I could continue to be angry. Lots of people told me how unfair my situation was, how this shouldn't be happening to me. It wasn't hard to justify continuing on that path.

But I hated how I felt. The anger wasn't who I wanted to be. It was taking too much control, and the path was dark ahead. Jesus was offering an alternative. The path he illuminated didn't show me the end, but it did offer a chance at peace. It would take trust on my part. Trust to place my anger in Jesus' hands and let him deal with it. Trust that God would stay with me. Trust in the plans God had for my life. Trust that no matter the future, belonging to Jesus would be enough.

Several years ago, I memorized Psalm 16:7 and 8. "I praise you Lord for being my guide. Even in the darkest night, your teachings fill my mind. I will always look to you, as you stand beside me and protect me from fear." (CEV) These verses had brought me through many situations. Now, in my darkest night, I had to decide if I really believed these verses. Was I going to allow God to fill my mind with his teachings? Could I keep my eyes on Jesus? Was God really standing beside me? Is it even possible to be protected from fear? I felt rocked to my core. How could these verses be true?

I've had many times in my life where I questioned God, and I always found he was able to not only handle my questions, but he kept close even in the questioning process. Now, when my questioning was at the deepest it had ever been, God brought those verses to my mind. I grabbed my Bible to read them again, and as I read, I noticed the following verse: "Therefore my heart is glad, and my tongue rejoices, and my body will also rest secure" (Psalm 16:9 NIV). It articulated exactly what I was longing for. I wanted my heart to be glad, the heaviness to lift, the anger to leave. I wanted my words to be full of thanks and praise to God, not complaints and rantings. My body was falling apart, and I was desperate to have some security for it. Could God really do all this? Was his Word really true?

It was in the middle of a very dark night I fell prostrate before God and repeated these verses over and over. I was pleading for a removal of the anger, a release from the powerful hold it had on me. Over and over, I repeated those verses. In doing so, I was submitting myself to God, my emotions, my words, and my health. I hung on, repeating the Scripture, begging God to do something. I asked God to make my heart glad, to help my tongue to be able to rejoice, to work in my body and heal it.

After a while I noticed my legs were asleep, and I made my way to a chair. While I waited for the feeling to return, I closed my eyes and took inventory of how I was feeling. I noticed that the heaviness of anger was gone. My mind wasn't swirling anymore. The thoughts were slower, more deliberate, without the accompanying angst that was there earlier. There was a small seed, deep in my soul, where I felt at peace.

In the days and weeks to follow, those verses were my mantra. When I woke at night, I would recite them. I began to combat sleeplessness by reading my Bible and praying. I changed the focus of my prayers during that time from myself to others. Slowly, I began to see sleeplessness as an opportunity to do something for others, to pray for them. I began to make lists, and when I couldn't sleep, I would pray for needs I was aware of. I also asked God to bring people to my mind who needed prayer. I noticed things on Facebook that people would share, about the hard stuff of life, and I added these to my list. The hours of sleeplessness became a very sweet time where God and I would talk.

I began to feel more rested through the days. This didn't really make sense, because I wasn't getting more sleep, but I was facing the days with a new perspective. The seed of peace that began with me face down on the floor sprouted with my daily surrender. My circumstances hadn't changed, but I was different. I knew it wasn't my work that was making this happen. Jesus was answering my prayer to make my heart glad and my tongue rejoice.

Getting to the end of ourselves is a painful process that most of us would rather avoid. I've always viewed myself as a strong person. Up to this point I'd met life's challenges and kept going. I assumed God had built me with some level of fortitude because I would need it. God was stripping away those assumptions I had made and revealing where I had allowed the strength he had created me with to creep into self-reliance. God was calling me to something new, a level of relationship with him I hadn't yet gone to. He was asking me to journey with him, to risk and see if he was enough.

God, I will be still and know that you are God.

You are my refuge and strength, an ever-present help in trouble. Therefore, I will not fear.

But as for me, I will always have hope; I will praise you more and more.

I praise you, Lord, for being my guide. Even in the darkest night, your teachings fill my mind. I will keep my eyes always on the Lord. With him at my right hand, I will not be shaken. Therefore, my heart is glad, and my tongue rejoices, and my body will also rest secure.

Chapter 5

Though you have made me see troubles,
many and bitter, you will restore my
life again; from the depths of the
earth you will again bring me up.
Psalm 71:20, NIV

With the anger released from my life, I no longer felt like I was drowning. My head felt above the surface, and I could breathe again. It was still a lot of work to keep myself afloat, but I didn't feel like I had to do it all by myself anymore. Jesus was with me, and I leaned into his strength.

The medical community continued to march onward with my treatment. A second surgery was on the horizon to remove the lump in my armpit. I was very anxious for this to happen. After all, this was the origin of the cancer. I wanted it gone! Covid was overwhelming the hospitals at this point, delaying all kinds of procedures. The surgeon was hopeful it would only be a few weeks to wait.

She tried to reassure me I was a top priority. I didn't actually find that reassuring at all. In the Covid context, only very serious cases were moving ahead with surgery.

That meant my prognosis was rather dire. I knew that. After all, the oncologist had told me to get my affairs in order, but I didn't want to face it. The idea my life would be shorter than expected was gut-wrenching, and I was trying to avoid thinking about it. Every time I was confronted with the reality of having stage 4 metastatic cancer, I wanted to turtle up, shoving my head into a dark space where the painful reality couldn't reach.

As I waited for the surgery date to arrive, I struggled to get through the days. My energy was returning, and I wanted to do something. Summer was arriving, my favorite time of year. I wanted to enjoy the warmth, the longer daylight. I tried to give some routine and purpose to my days. I spent my mornings reading, praying, reflecting, and journaling. The nice weather allowed outside visits, and these were wonderful. Sitting with people and talking, while socially distanced to keep safe from Covid, gave me the connection I longed for. But even as I talked with my family and friends there was something missing. I couldn't quite put my finger on it. It felt as though I was observing everything instead of experiencing it. The connections weren't quite making it all the way. A sadness deep in my soul took hold. As much as my family and friends loved me, would do anything for me, were demonstrating their love for me, I felt alone. Looking at my emotions objectively, it didn't make sense. How could someone with so much support in their life feel so alone?

I tried to pray about it, but it was a struggle to even articulate. I just couldn't put into words the loneliness I felt. The prayers were simple. *Lord, help me. I don't feel right. Something just isn't right.* I kept reading my Bible. If I didn't keep this discipline, I knew I would go back under. Treading water became very tiresome and so, so lonely. My husband noticed the sadness. He tried to help in many ways. I did my best to smile, because I knew he was trying so hard to help me. It broke my heart that I couldn't connect with him, to help him understand how I felt. There's an expression that says, "If you feel like you're at the end of your rope, tie a knot and hang on." That's what I did. I tied the biggest knot I could, grabbed on with both hands, and hung on.

The day arrived for my second surgery. It came quicker than my surgeon predicted. I knew God was working, answering prayers to speed up the process. Covid delays hadn't changed, but I was getting through the necessary medical process quicker than I should have. I was very thankful for this. I was desperate to get the lump out of me! The procedure was day surgery. I was so grateful not to have to spend a long time in the hospital again. Saying goodbye to my husband that morning and walking back into the hospital by myself was hard. Fear crept into the edges of my mind. All the possible complications popped into my mind. It was once again a battle, and it felt like an attack. I prayed and recited Scripture through all the preparations. When the time came for them to put me under, I was very peaceful. Jesus was right there by my side.

The surgeon was very confident. "I was able to get the whole thing." Sweet words broke through the haze as I woke from the anesthesia. I don't react well to anesthetic. It takes a very long time for me to kick it out of my system. They had woken me up several times, but each time I couldn't keep my eyes open. Nausea complicated the process. Any slight movement sent me over the edge.

It took much longer than expected before I could be released. I didn't have any sense of time, so I had no idea Keith had been waiting much longer than expected. That was another nasty part of Covid. Those who are waiting outside the hospital don't have a full picture of what is happening on the inside. In a normal environment, Keith could have been with me while I recovered. He would have been reassured I was okay, just needing extra time to wake up. Instead, he had to pass the time in worry and uncertainty. It was so brutally unfair for him. When the medical team finally wheeled me out to our vehicle, I could see the burden of the wait on his countenance. His appearance sagged, a heavy emotional weight. Once again, the reality of his journey with me pierced my heart.

Recovery from soft-tissue surgery is much different than brain surgery. I found it to be much more painful. Movement was a significant challenge, and the physiotherapy, while necessary, was hard and painful work. It took determination to do the exercises I needed to do. Repetition was the key but motivation to move my body through painful exercise was low. At times I would become angry with Keith for reminding me to do the work. I wanted an instant recovery, an immediate return of normal function to my body.

I was still lonely. As much as Keith walked with me, he couldn't know how my body felt, both physically and emotionally. I knew he sensed my distance, but I didn't have a clue how to bridge the gap. Each day I would wake up and beg God to help me get through the day, the pain, the challenges, the loneliness.

One evening, Keith and I were watching a movie we had recorded. When it was over, the PVR switched to television, and there was a show on with a woman talking about her cancer journey. Keith moved on to something else, but I sat riveted to the TV. This woman was talking about her journey of first losing a mom and sister to cancer, and then getting her own diagnosis. As she described her journey, every word mirrored my own feelings. It was like she was talking right to me. Her words, her description of her feelings and reactions, were exactly what I had been struggling to articulate for weeks. Here was someone talking about their cancer journey, and they were just like me. Someone else who had the same experience.

After the interview was over, I went to bed but couldn't sleep. I had to find out more. I got on the computer and looked up the person interviewed on the show, Nicky Hardy. I read about her cancer journey, found her website, ordered her book, and subscribed to her podcasts. The words I read were so comforting because it was someone else who knew what the cancer journey was like. It connected with me. Once I finally crawled back into bed that night, I felt so different.

After such unique encouragement, I didn't feel so alone. I had resources to help with my own journey. As I thanked God for finding this, it hit me. I didn't find this; God sent it. Pondering the circumstances, I could see Jesus' fingerprints. The movie we chose to start watching ended at the moment the interview was being aired. The channel on the TV didn't need to be changed. I didn't go looking for something to watch. I was done with TV for the night. Before I had a chance to shut down the screen, the words of the interview caught my attention.

This was a direct answer to my desperate prayers. I felt so alone, and God connected me with someone who understood exactly what I was going through and had created resources to help. He had arranged for me to see the interview on the TV exactly when I needed it. It was like he whispered in my ear, *"Here you go, Heather. I've heard you asking for help and I've arranged for someone to give you some things you need. I've still got you."* Realizing this, I crept out of bed again, and knelt, only this time it wasn't in desperation, but rather overwhelming thanksgiving for the way in which Jesus provided for me. It was such a tender, beautiful answer to the desperate longing of my heart. I knew, once again, God was going to be enough.

Restoration is a process. Anyone who has taken something and restored it will understand things look pretty messy for a long time before they begin to look good again. That's kind of how my summer went. When I looked in the mirror, I didn't recognize myself. My face was round and puffy from the medication. My body sagged everywhere, and the dark circles under my eyes were pronounced. My hair had begun to fall out. Handfuls in the shower drain, the bathroom floor always full of hair. It revealed the massive scar that was still healing on my skull.

I had to use a mirror to see that scar, and when I did, I found it huge, ugly, and nasty. I didn't want to look at it, and I sure didn't want people to see it. It was so pronounced it was hard to ignore. I wore a hat whenever I went out. As the hair continued to fall out, I realized it would be awhile before anything would look even remotely normal on my head. I was very self-conscious of the scar and finally made the decision to get a wig.

This proved to be an interesting process, new and uncomfortable. I found a very kind woman, who gently took me through the process to find something to suit me and that I felt comfortable with. She also showed me different wraps and buffs I could use. I came home from the appointment a little encouraged. I showed the wig off to my sons, sent a few pics to some trusted friends. It was a little slice of feeling like I was getting back to myself.

One day as I was piddling around the house, I caught sight of myself in the mirror and it hit me. There I was, head wrapped up, loose clothes, unfamiliar face. *I look like a cancer patient!* This shouldn't have been such a shock because I was a cancer patient. It was my reality once again bursting onto the scene. That's what I have found it to be like having cancer. You can be going about your day, and suddenly, *bam*, the reality of cancer shouts down everything and demands attention. My life had been altered forever. I would never be able to go back to life like it was. I found this to be overwhelmingly sad. I had loved the life I had, and cancer showed up and ripped it apart.

It didn't just affect me; it changed things for Keith and our sons too. Uncertainty was now an uninvited guest we were all trying to tolerate but desperately wished would just leave. Trying to distract myself from it proved pointless, because it never left. No matter what I did, no matter who I was with, deep down I was just sad. This was strange for me. I had never felt like this before.

Every day there was this battle within me. I would wake thankful for another day, thankful for life, thankful for the many blessings that were part of my life. And every day I would also wake with the weight deep within, an overwhelming sense of loss. These two things would battle through the day. When I was by myself, the sadness would wash over like a wave and soak me. When I was around people, I was so grateful not to be alone. It felt like I was pushing a giant boulder up a hill and every time I got a few feet up, my strength would fail, and that boulder would roll right back over me, leaving me flat, empty, and exhausted.

One day, sitting in yet another examination room waiting for the oncologist, I noticed a poster on the wall. It had a peaceful and serene picture of a path. As I stared at the picture, I noticed the words at the bottom. "Help for the journey." I wondered what it was about. I sure needed help for my journey. When the doctor came in, I asked her about it. The poster was for the Psychosocial Oncology Department. I didn't even know such a thing existed. I sure needed someone to talk to about everything, so I called.

Support groups weren't running, and resources were limited due to the pandemic, but I was able to get connected with a social worker. Virtual visits were the only thing available. It was a little awkward at first, but she was very kind and insightful, and I was able to feel like I finally had someone to talk to. Getting connected with this social worker was an answer to prayer. My family and friends were supportive and always there for me, but there were things I couldn't say to them, fears, and thoughts I wasn't even sure I should say out loud, let alone to someone close to me. The social worker was a safe place to voice those thoughts and feelings. She listened and guided, assuring me everything I was experiencing was normal.

I was going through a period of grieving, and all the stages that go with it. I grieved the loss of the life I had known. I hadn't thought of it like that. I thought I was being ungrateful when I was angry or sad. After all, I was still alive. Shouldn't I just be grateful and move forward? But this was not how the process goes, and she helped me understand what I was going through. Together we were able to identify things, and I didn't feel so lost anymore.

The thing about grief is there isn't a short cut. You don't get to skip over the unpleasant stuff. It's not like the game Snakes and Ladders, where you get to jump ahead if you can just land on the right spot. I was going to have to walk this path of grief, one step at a time. Facing my feelings, recognizing them, working through them was the only way forward. It was hard work. When sadness would rise, I would turn and face the emotion, name it, and give myself permission to experience the moment. Not getting lost in the process was difficult. I went from not understanding what I was experiencing to facing all the loss associated with cancer and trying not to allow it to take me down.

My time in prayer was not very joyful, and praise was tough. It felt a little mechanical to praise God when it was so disconnected from my emotions. I'd love to say I just prayed, and everything turned around right away. That wasn't the case. But I kept on reading my Bible and talking to Jesus. I knew he was really close. I knew he was walking with me, but I still felt so sad.

Reading my Bible one day, I came upon Psalm 71:20. "Though you have made me see troubles, many and bitter, you will restore my life again; from the depths of the earth you will again bring me up." (Psalm 71:20, NIV) Well, my troubles sure were many and bitter. Cancer changed the trajectory of my life, taking my spirit, dictating my emotions, shattering my dreams, ruining my hope. This was bitter trouble. The first part of the verse brought up my distress. "Though you have made me see troubles." *Why didn't you stop this, Jesus? Why does this have to be my life? What is the point of all this?* Once again, I had lots of questions without any clear answers.

The middle part of the verse made me begin to wonder. *Will God restore me? Can God restore me? Of course he can, he's God. Nothing is impossible for him. Will he do it? Should*

I ask for it? Do I dare? You see, in my despair and grief, I didn't feel worthy enough to ask Jesus to restore my life. The grief had taken me to a dark place, where I assumed I would stay. I couldn't see a way out, but this verse stuck in my mind like a seed that sticks in your tooth. It grabs your attention, and even if you try to focus on something else, you always go back to that little seed, and you work away at it until you can free it. God restoring my life became something I couldn't get out of my mind. Somewhere in the middle of the grief, God used this verse to plant a tiny seed of hope. It got stuck in my mind, and I turned it over and over again. *Do I dare ask for this?*

I wanted to desperately but wasn't sure if I should be bold enough. That may seem ridiculous to an outsider, but when you are struggling in a dark place, where sadness and grief have taken over, it's hard to be able to reach out. *Please, Jesus, please.* That was all I could do. I cried out in my spirit, and I believe God's spirit intervened for me and took my cries right to the Father. Scripture says the Spirit intercedes for us with groanings. (Romans 8:26, ESV) I believe this is what God did for me.

I read the verse daily, first in my mind, and then whispered it. It was like I needed courage to be able to speak it out loud. Slowly, very slowly, there was a small crack in the wall of sadness enveloping me. I kept repeating this verse. The more I said it, the more I believed it. It wasn't just that I needed to believe those words, but in saying them I surrendered to what was taking place. I laid down the future I had hoped to have and surrendered my future to God. The grief led me through a journey of anger, despair, sadness, bargaining with God.

Once I had gone through all those, I faced accepting the path God had me on. Could I accept this? Would I accept this? It was both the will and heart that had to accept where I was at. I had to accept cancer was now part of my life and had to accept I was still in God's hands. I had never experienced a surrender like this, and my will fought it, but I cried out to Jesus. *Jesus, I do want to surrender, but my will is holding on. Please break that.* God was asking me to surrender my life, however it would play out, to him.

It was scary because life now included this life-threatening disease. When it came right down to it, I had no other choice. Living without Jesus wouldn't be living. So, I asked Jesus to show me how to surrender. It was a painful, gut-wrenching, laying down of my life on a level I didn't even know existed. Jesus held me the whole time, gave me strength, comforted me, allowed the tears and anguish, and then washed comfort and peace over me. It was settled. I would take the troubles, many and bitter, and wait for him to restore my life. I didn't know if restoration would happen on earth or in heaven, but I knew God would be faithful and do what he promised. God was still enough.

God, I will be still and know that you are God.

You are my refuge and strength, an ever-present help in trouble. Therefore, I will not fear.

But as for me, I will always have hope; I will praise you more and more.

I praise you, Lord, for being my guide. Even in the darkest night, your teachings fill my mind. I will keep my eyes always on the Lord. With him at my right hand, I will not be shaken. Therefore, my heart is glad, and my tongue rejoices, and my body will also rest secure.

Though you have made me see troubles, many and bitter, you will restore my life again, from the depths of the earth you will again bring me up.

Chapter 6

But I trust in you, Lord; I say, "You are my God." My times are in your hands ... Let your face shine on your servant; save me in your unfailing love. Let me not be put to shame, Lord, for I have cried out to you.
Psalm 31:14-15a, 16–17a, NIV

A lot of us have moments when the direction of our life changes. A new course is set, and it brings a whole new group of circumstances. Sometimes we can see these moments arriving, such as graduation from a particular course of study. A lot of effort and time is spent getting to the end of the studies, and then the direction changes and we set off on another adventure. Maybe the direction is more education, such as when someone graduates from high school and decides to pursue post-secondary education. Or the direction could be entering the workforce and learning how to navigate in a new arena. Either direction is full of possibilities and maybe some uncertainty, but it is a planned change in the course of our life, and we are prepared for and expect the challenges that come with it. We move forward with the new direction from a place of readiness.

Other moments might not be so certain, but they are still on our radar, such as a marriage proposal. Relationships are tricky and not always certain, because we aren't in complete control. There is another person involved who has both influence and power over the direction the relationship takes. There might be a lot of indications, signals, and signs a relationship is headed towards permanency in marriage, but until someone proposes and the I do's are said, we don't know for certain if this is where we will end up. There is still a lot we can do to influence the direction of the relationship though, and it brings comfort. We want that change in direction. The uncertainty exists, but we hold it in tension with our wants and desires, and this becomes a manageable uncertainty.

Then there are the times when life's direction changes without our planning, without our input. I remember when my family made a move when I was growing up. It was only a move across the city, but to a ten-year-old, that was moving to a whole new world. The circumstances of my life, friends, school, and neighborhood were all going to change. It was a big deal. Later on, with my own family, we made some moves with our children. The biggest was from Cambridge to a city six hours away, Ottawa. This uprooted our sons' lives. They only knew one city, one school, one set of friends and activities.

As we made the long drive to our new city, I watched in the rearview mirror as our kids stared out the window with the saddest faces I had ever seen on them. It broke my heart. I knew I couldn't take the pain away, and as parents we were responsible for it. I also knew they would get through it; they would make new friends, we would have new experiences as a family, and life would go on. It was a change, but it wasn't the end. I knew that, but they didn't. They could only see everything was changing and they didn't have control over it. Their pain was real. Uncertainty ruled their lives.

When unexpected and unwanted change happens, when circumstances are dictated to us, it's painful. The control is gone, and it feels like life is spinning. We land in new and frightening territory and wonder how this will ever work out. I remember reading something shortly after my diagnosis. I don't remember where I read it, but I remember my reaction very clearly. I was inundated with all kinds of medical procedures at the time and trying to remember what appointment was when. I suddenly had a team of doctors, and for someone who had only ever dealt with a family physician, it was overwhelming. I felt like I was barely keeping up. My mind, my thoughts, my emotions were barely holding things together, and the feeling of being on the edge was very real. One day, while reading I came across these words: "God's plan for your life is your best possible outcome."

The word "outcome" was another nagging seed in my tooth that wouldn't come out. It irritated me and kept bringing my mind and focus back to it. There had been lots of talk about outcomes for me. The whole focus of my treatment plan was based on what kind of outcome could be expected. Various doctors talked about what kind of outcome we could expect from the different treatments. These weren't very positive conversations, and I was always kind of depressed after them. So, when I read my best possible outcome was God's plan, I reacted negatively. *Well, that's just a load of crap! I need something better than God's plan, because I'm stuck fighting cancer right now, and this can't be his plan. If his plan is this, then I don't want it.* My lack of understanding, my inability to see the big picture, dictated my reactions. I was being driven away from my life, the life I knew, took comfort in, had plans for.

One of the biggest roadblocks for me was my family. I desperately didn't want my loved ones to have this pain. How could God allow this to happen to them? Keith and I had spent twenty-six years in pastoral ministry. There was great joy and pain in that service, but we knew we were serving God like he asked, and that brought peace. Our three sons were just getting launched into adulthood, navigating the world and all the challenges that come with that. Our family had faced stresses to relationships and the heartache that can come with family life.

I felt like we had just turned a corner and were heading in a positive direction. Now cancer had come and blown all that into tiny pieces. Nothing made sense. Life was in shambles, and every time I looked into one of their faces, all I could see was pain. I hated that with every fiber of my being. I wanted the pain to be gone! How could God do this to us? Why was God doing this to us? This can't be the best possible outcome!

Sessions with my social worker from the cancer center eventually included discussions about my family. One of the hardest parts of the process was dealing with how I felt about my family. I would plead every day with God to not let me die, so Keith and the boys wouldn't have that pain. I didn't care about me. If I died, I knew I would be with Jesus and so I wouldn't have anything painful at all. But I just couldn't get past what that would do to my family. I didn't want that pain for them. I pleaded with God to keep it from them. I told him they needed me. Keith and I should be allowed to have time together after our sons are on their own. Our sons should have a mom to cheer them on as they get into jobs and lives and families. I should be able to meet my grandkids. It's funny. I never really gave a lot of thought to having grandkids until the idea was put in jeopardy. Then I realized how mad and sad I was it might not happen. I begged and pleaded with God to please let me have a future because my family needed me. They were all guys after all and needed me to keep things together.

I kind of got stuck in a cycle. Each day I would spend time reading my Bible and praying. It would end with me on the floor, begging God to spare my family from the pain of losing me. This went on for a few weeks. As I talked with my social worker about it, she explained I was grieving the loss of my future. Before cancer, I lived in the assumption I had a future. Now the future was nothing but uncertainty. This was a painful realization, one I resisted making for a while. I just didn't want to go there. Yet I knew deep down it was a place of surrender God was calling me to.

One day, as I lay weeping on the floor yet again, God got hold of my thoughts. I was at the end of myself, all cried out, and my mind was still. In that moment God whispered, "Heather, don't you think I am capable of taking care of your family, even without you here?" Those words cut deep. I realized I wasn't trusting God with my family. I wanted to be the one to have control, take care of them, and I wasn't surrendering them to God. I was holding on. Fear had me paralyzed. In the quietness of the moment, God stripped bare all of my assumptions, exposed my arrogance, and challenged the premise of my thinking. I was faced with a decision. Was I going to trust my family to God? Was I going to surrender the control I was trying to keep? Was I willing to let him be in charge of my family?

I felt so ashamed. God had been providing for me and my family through decades. Why did I think he needed me around to continue to care for them? God was in charge, and I was interfering in that. He could provide everything they needed, care for them, give them exactly what they needed without me. If they were going to lose me, God would be enough for that pain too. I had to let them go, release them into his care, and trust he was enough for them. Releasing them to God was something I couldn't do on my own, but God led me through a process allowing me to get to the point I could let go. It was a painful but necessary process.

So much of my identity was wrapped up in being a wife and a mom. I loved it, felt it was what I was made to do. But in living out that gifting I somehow made it into something that was mine instead of God's. I took his gift, wrapped it up in my own expectations, and then wouldn't let him have it back. Now, God was asking for it back again. It was never really mine to begin with, but I had convinced myself it was. When I finally let go of the hold I had on my family, I felt such peace. A weight was lifted. The struggle was gone, and the surrender gave me freedom. I realized I hadn't lost anything. I had given full control back to God of the thing he had blessed me with for so many years. With the surrendering of that control came peace. My trust that God was going to be enough for my family grew. I now had a confidence he was taking care of them on a level I didn't need to understand, just trust in.

"But I trust in you, Lord; I say, 'You are my God.' My times are in your hands ... Let your face shine on your servant; save me in your unfailing love. Let me not be put to shame Lord, for I have cried out to you" (Psalm 31:14-15a, 16–17a, NIV). In my crying out to God, he did not fail. He showed me how to trust him on a level I didn't know was possible. God saw my pain like a parent sees the pain of their child. He knew my heart was breaking, and it broke his heart too. He knew the surrender that needed to happen, and he was so loving as he took me through that process. He never turned back or left me on my own.

I didn't understand what he was doing, but I felt his love through it all. In the middle of my pain, Jesus let his face shine on me. He saved me in his unfailing love. He saw me in the rearview mirror as we were traveling down the road, and he reached into my heart and held it as it broke, and then repaired the break with his peace and love. My control was like walls that had to be broken through to get at the treasure of peace that was waiting inside. Jesus was waiting there, at the very center of my being, just waiting for the walls to come down so I could discover he was at the center of everything, that I could trust him with everything. When I cried out to him, he answered. With all the guarantees of life gone, God gave me a certainty in him that he was enough, and he would *be* enough.

Now I can pray with confidence that my times are in his hands. It's not about the circumstances changing. The change was within me. I didn't make the change myself; I couldn't. What I could do is surrender to God the most precious thing I had, my family. He took that surrender and reassured me he was enough for it. He was in control. I truly don't know what lies ahead, but I am now equipped to trust God with all the challenges that lie ahead of me. I recite those verses from Psalm 31 often. I need God's help every single day to trust him. He is faithfully doing the work. I feel the warmth of his smile, and I know he is enough for this journey.

What about you? Up to now I've been doing all the sharing, trying to convey my experiences. I'm not unique though. If we were sitting having coffee it would be time for me to begin asking you some questions. Your story has its own set of unique challenging circumstances. I'd like to invite you to reflect on where things are in your life. I don't know the circumstances of your life, the heartaches, the pain deep within you. When the relationship ends, when the layoff happens, when your child is sick, when debt sinks you, when mental illness takes a family member down a dark path, when death snatches someone away, fill in your own circumstance. The list of possibilities is so brutally long. In the middle of the painful agony, what do you believe?

When the direction of your life changes, what is your response? I'm not glossing over anything here. These are tough, challenging questions, and I am not making light of the circumstances. No pat answers here, no stupid quotes that make light of the situation. I can only offer you what I have learned. In the middle of your utter painful brokenness, Jesus sees your pain, knows it's real, feels everything you feel, and it breaks his heart too. He loves you that much. He is right there in it with you. When every guarantee you have held onto crumbles in your hands, Jesus is the guarantee that doesn't fade. I am absolutely convinced because I have experienced it. I am certain Jesus is enough. He is still there when all the guarantees of life are gone. That's because he is the only real guarantee. He promises over and over in his word that he will be with you, never leave you. I have found this to be true in the most challenging, painful, and confusing circumstances. Jesus' love never stops. His presence truly is enough. Releasing the control, the grip we have on our life, allows us to honestly put our times in his hands, and discover Jesus is enough.

God, I will be still and know that you are God.

You are my refuge and strength, an ever-present help in trouble. Therefore, I will not fear.

But as for me, I will always have hope; I will praise you more and more.

I praise you, Lord, for being my guide. Even in the darkest night, your teachings fill my mind. I will keep my eyes always on the Lord. With him at my right hand I will not be shaken. Therefore, my heart is glad, and my tongue rejoices, and my body will also rest secure.

Though you have made me see troubles, many and bitter, you will restore my life again, from the depths of the earth you will again bring me up.

Lord, in all the challenges that lie ahead, help me to trust in you. My times are in your hands. Let your face shine on your servant; save me in your unfailing love. Let me not be put to shame, Lord, for I have cried out to you.

Chapter 7

Give your entire attention to what God is
doing right now, and don't get worked up
about what may or may not happen tomorrow.
God will help you deal with whatever hard
things come up when the time comes.
Matthew 6:34, MSG

Growing up, I always enjoyed physical activities. Different sports and games were a source of enjoyment. Swimming was my favorite, and I spent many hours in the pool. I went through lessons, lifeguard training, and eventually ended up in synchronized swimming. This was really fun. I loved being able to move through the water in unique ways, the challenge of learning to hold my breath for long periods of time, and working with a team to swim in unison.

In order to stay synchronized, we had to be able to hear the beat of music under the water. That constant run of eight guided every movement. To practice, the coach would hold a metal pole in the water and bang against the pole. The sound would travel under the water, and we would hear it and move to the beat. Then the music would be piped through the underwater speaker, and this would allow us to refine our movements. The beat gave us direction and kept us on track. It was always there. If you lost count, you could always listen carefully and find the beginning of the run of eight to get back on track.

It was also crucial to use your teammates to keep on track. We always had to be aware of where everyone was, and where everyone was heading. You used your teammates to keep your spot in the formation precisely where it should be. This took trust. You couldn't see from above to know if you were out of formation, so you had to rely on everyone using the point of reference their teammate provided to get things right. We never saw the formations from above, but we knew where we were supposed to be and trusted everyone was also where they should be. We worked as a team to create something that was only seen from outside the team. Our perspective in the water was limited, but we knew we were creating something that would be seen from above.

When I got cancer, my perspective on life radically changed. I was suddenly living a life dictated by uncertainty. I was involved in the medical world in ways that were new and unfamiliar. I had to figure out how to navigate this new world. It was like I had lost the beat of my life. I was used to living my life with a certain beat and rhythm, and suddenly I just couldn't hear the beat anymore. As hard as I listened, it just wasn't there. It felt directionless and scary.

There were a whole bunch of new people in my life now, directing my treatment and care. Each appointment, each conversation, I tried to figure out how things work in that world, but I only had bits and pieces. We always tried to have Keith on speakerphone for the conversations with the doctors. This was a challenge. Cancer centers are full of all kinds of equipment that interfere with cellular signals, and we could never count on the connection happening, or being clear if it did go through. I found this to be so frustrating.

The information I got at appointments was crucial to have and remember. I would listen carefully, take notes, and try so hard to get everything clear in my head. The problem was the emotional stress of the situation would cause my mind to get things jumbled. Sometimes the doctor would just say a few certain words, and the anxiety and stress hearing those words caused would make my mind get fuzzy. It would be hard to concentrate and focus on what was coming for the rest of the appointment.

If Keith couldn't get connected through the call, and we had to rely on my notes, we chanced missing something. Then I would feel like I let Keith down, because I couldn't answer his questions. Guilt would just compound all the stress, and I would kind of shut down for a bit. It was like I just couldn't handle processing the information and my mind would hit the overload point. If Keith could just go to the appointments with me, we wouldn't have the problem, but it was never an option. Covid saw to that.

I knew I wasn't alone in any of my cancer journey. I had a husband and three sons who were there for me in both practical and emotionally supportive ways. They would get things at the store I needed, patiently trying to figure out exactly what my lists meant. They helped with tasks around the house, reducing the demands on me so I could prioritize my health and build physical strength slowly. I needed to work at different cognitive tasks as well as physical. Ones that would challenge my brain in various ways. I worked on puzzles, crafts, and word games on my own. It was often a slow process.

Our youngest still lived at home, and he and Keith patiently sat through numerous card games. It took a long time for me to decide what card to play. My brain was slow to engage in complex decision making, and even simple games were a challenge. Often, I would play a card after a long pause, feeling like I had finally figured things out correctly, and one of them would gently ask me if I really wanted to play that card. I was making errors but couldn't see it. I love playing games and am often the one coaxing my guys into playing. It was maddening to have something I love become so difficult. It also brought a stark realization of the depth of the injury my brain had suffered.

My parents lived nearby, and they were available for whatever we needed. We chatted a lot, breaking up my long days. They would show up at the door with a delicious meal. As my strength grew, they would take me to their place for the day. This provided a chance up get out of my house and distract myself from the realities of cancer. They were generous in their loving support.

There were so many friends who also supported me. They would come and spend time, had coffee with me virtually, and kept checking in on how I was doing. Even with all the restrictions and cautions we needed to take in the midst of the pandemic, people were incredibly creative in how they demonstrated their support. I'll never forget answering the doorbell one day to find a group of work friends spaced out on my front lawn and down the street, all waving at me and shouting encouragement.

Then there were all the medical professionals who were suddenly part of our lives. God arranged the care of a host of doctors during a time when access to medical services was being severely limited. Add these to the family and friends, and I should have felt grateful for such an amazing team of people in my life. I did on an intellectual level. Logically, in my thought process, I was very grateful, but my emotions weren't matching up. While I knew I was grateful, I also had immense feelings of loneliness and sadness. It seemed a paradox to feel so grateful and lonely at the same time. My perspective was skewed.

It felt like I was lost in a bad synchro routine. I was swimming around, going to all the points that used to be a reference for me, only to find they didn't exist anymore. The team was still there, but I didn't know how to use them to find where I should be. I didn't trust they would know what I needed, because no one fully understood what I was going through. I could sort of hear a beat, but I couldn't find the top of the count. I kept trying but would get so frustrated.

I had always considered myself someone who could handle stressful situations. After all, between teaching and being married to a pastor, stress was a daily reality. Situations came at me from all angles, and I was used to changing directions quickly, adapting to the new circumstance. Cancer was a new and unfamiliar kind of stress. I wanted to meet the challenge and face the stress, but I felt like it kept getting the better of me. I didn't have a frame of reference to interpret all the new interactions I was having with the medical community, and misinterpretation would add to the anxiety and stress. It felt like I was swimming with a brand-new team and I couldn't hear the music.

As the summer rolled on, there wasn't the usual excitement for me. I love the season, the long, lazy, warm days. This time, I felt a lot of anxiety. The sun was suddenly my enemy. I was never one to sit out in the sun for long periods of time. I have fair skin, which burns easily, so I always had to keep sunscreen on. Now, with a diagnosis of melanoma, I didn't know how to navigate. I felt like the cancer was my own fault. I probably didn't take enough caution. I thought of all the times I did get a burn. The times when I lathered up but missed a tiny spot and got burned. Times I thought I was okay because I was in the shade, but now I knew the sun was still damaging me even when I didn't get burned. I felt like I had caused this, and regret sat very heavy. How was I supposed to enjoy being outside?

I was trying to get regular exercise by going for walks. Initially I was only able to get to the end of the block, but slowly my endurance improved. At first someone had to go with me because I was quite unsteady on my feet, and I tired easily. Keith and I would walk hand in hand, and I remember my neighbor commenting on how sweet it was. If she only knew I had to hold his hand to keep from falling over! Our two oldest sons would visit, and I would joke with them that they could take their mom for a walk like they used to take the dog. As my strength grew, I was able to get out on my own, and I would walk through a forest path close by. I did lap after lap of the area, and as I walked, I would often talk to God. Some days it was a quiet conversation where I could see and hear him through creation. Other days it was a rant of all the pain, frustration, and uncertainty I lived with. I really wanted the rhythm of my life back. The one I knew, was familiar with. That's what I was listening for but couldn't find. Would I ever hear it again?

"Give your entire attention to what God is doing right now, and don't get worked up about what may or may not happen tomorrow. God will help you deal with whatever hard things come up when the time comes." (Matthew 6:34, MSG) I came across the verse during this time of turmoil. What a challenge! Could I really live this way? I couldn't get the thoughts out of my head. I was familiar with the verse in another version. "Therefore, do not worry about tomorrow, for tomorrow will worry about itself. Each day has enough trouble of its own." (Matthew 6:34, NIV) I had heard it being used as a pat answer to give people when they were going through a hard time. It seemed like a formula being applied rather than a certainty you could build your life on. *Just don't worry. Easy to say when you don't have a stage 4 diagnosis. I need something realistic, something I can hang on to with both hands.*

When I read this verse in *The Message*, God grabbed my attention and said, "Heather, listen up! This is for you. I've got an answer for your desperate prayers." I pondered each part of the verse. What was God doing right now? I did really believe he was with me. There was too much evidence not to believe that. I had experienced him so powerfully I couldn't disbelieve in his presence. What was Jesus up to though? How do I reconcile my circumstances to the idea that God is doing something when it doesn't make any sense to my human mind?

The whole "don't get worked up about what may or may not happen" was a colossal challenge. How was I supposed to not get worked up? The doctor had told me to get my affairs in order. The prognosis was not great. Even with successful surgeries, the five-year survival rate for my type of cancer was grim. I had done some research. Recurrence rates with melanoma tend to be high, especially with later stages. I may not have a whole lot of tomorrows. Wasn't that something I was allowed to get worked up about? The hard things that might come made for a long list: uncertainty, emotional and physical pain, grief, loss of all the things I thought I would get to have and do in my life. Where was the sense in this verse? Was I really supposed to believe it was possible? How could I figure out how to trust Jesus with the future? In the hollowness of my uncertainty, could I trust God with whatever would or would not happen? The whole "may or may not happen" part was tricky. No one really knew what was ahead for me, not even the medical community. That's why I was living with uncertainty.

We all live with uncertainty, after all no one knows for certain what will happen tomorrow. There is a certain assumption tomorrow will come, and we live in that. We kind of have to. After all, if we spent our lives fixated on the uncertainty it would take us to dark and depressing places, allowing anxiety to crush us. My new circumstances were forcing me to examine how I lived my life, and what I would do with the uncertainty.

So, what was God doing right then? How could I get my focus on the immediate, the present? Getting brutally honest with myself, I knew I couldn't do this in my own power. The weight of my circumstances was just too heavy. I was being crushed under the burden of it all. It permeated my days in ways that made each one a real struggle. I would resolve each new day to keep my mind positive, focused on the blessing in store the day. But it was never long before the negative, fearful thoughts would arrive. I began to pray this verse, asking God to help me give my entire attention to what he was doing. *Let me see what you are up to in my life. Help me to learn this new routine, this new rhythm of life. I need to hear your beat through all of this other noise that keeps crowding my mind and emotions.*

I prayed the verse every day, often several times a day. Sometimes it came easily to pray, and other times it took every ounce of energy to be able to say the words. So much of the time it was like a battle, and those words were the weapons. It would exhaust me emotionally, but I kept at it. I was desperate to understand. I needed to understand to be able to keep going.

I was reminded of what it was like when I was learning a new routine at synchro. We would first spend long periods of time learning the routine on land. The continual drilling, counting, and learning the reference points took a lot of time. We didn't even get into the water some days until the last little bit of the practice. As I thought about that, I realized I was in a time of learning a new routine. It was hard, felt awkward. It took so much focus just to keep listening to the beat and counting. I had new reference points to keep my eyes on. I had to repeat things over and over. God was teaching me a new routine for my life, and it would take hard work and perseverance to learn.

It didn't happen overnight, but as I continued to practice and put my efforts into learning this new routine, there was a change in my perspective over the summer. During my times of walking, I noticed more of my surroundings, the beauty in creation, the people who were out walking, the building strength in my body. I began to spend more and more time reading the Bible and studying it. I intentionally did some studying on prayer and learned a lot from Jesus' example. When I was with family or friends, I was able to concentrate more on what they were saying, and surprisingly, I found ways to also encourage them.

I had opportunities to share my testimony with two small groups. This was something I wasn't sure I could do. How could I possibly convey what God was doing in my life, when I was still working that out every day? But God met me in my neediness, and gave me the words and the strength to share them. In being obedient to share, I found strength. I was able to find comfort in being vulnerable with other people. This was something very new for me. A part of my new routine.

Praying Matthew 6:34 over and over did not go unanswered. God showed me how to embrace each new day and look for the blessings he had waiting for me in it. He taught me a new rhythm for life. The cry of my heart, for understanding, came through a change in my perspective. I could find peace in living each day, just as it came. I had a new routine I was continuing to learn. My confidence that Jesus would give me the strength for the hard things, whenever they might show up, grew. I believed that more each day. My circumstances didn't change, my perspective did. Each day arrived with opportunities, and if I allowed God to give me focus, then I would find what he had waiting for me.

One day, while walking, it struck me that I was different. The turmoil wasn't there. The work of learning a new routine, while invisible to begin with, broke through. A new kind of life appeared. I had found a new beat and rhythm for my life. The nourishment I found every day in Scripture allowed me to live with real peace. I could hear Jesus tapping out the beat, keeping me steady in his rhythm. And in that rhythm was strength, peace, and comfort because I knew I would always have everything I needed in Jesus and his love for me. He was enough.

I will be still and know that you are God.

You are my refuge and strength, an ever-present help in trouble. Therefore, I will not fear.

But as for me, I will always have hope; I will praise you more and more.

I praise you Lord for being my guide. Even in the darkest night, your teachings fill my mind. I will keep my eyes always on the Lord. With him at my right hand, I will not be shaken. Therefore, my heart is glad, and my tongue rejoices, and my body will also rest secure.

Though you have made me see troubles, many and bitter, you will restore my life again, from the depths of the earth you will again bring me up.

Lord, in all the challenges that lie ahead, help me to trust in you. My times are in your hands ... Let your face shine on your servant; save me in your unfailing love. Let me not be put to shame, Lord, for I have cried out to you.

Help me to give my entire attention to what you are doing right now and not get worked up about what may or may not happen tomorrow. I claim the promise that God will help me deal with whatever hard things come up when the time comes.

Chapter 8

Do not be afraid or discouraged, for the Lord
will personally go ahead of you. He will be with
you; he will neither fail you nor abandon you.
Deuteronomy 31:8, NLT

Whate does discouragement look like for you? With me, I don't always recognize discouragement. Some days I'm just in a mood. Nothing is going my way. Tiny obstacles grow exponentially. There is a general feeling of discontent. My mind is swirling around something, but I can't get a clear picture. It's like looking at something through water. I can see the outline, some colors, and sort of the shape, but nothing is clear. I should be able to just reach down and pull the object out of the water, but instead I just keep staring at it.

Discouragement in my cancer journey was a constant enemy. It battled against my energy, my resources, and so many times it won. For several months the battle raged. I would wake up and resolve to have a positive day. I would fix my mind on the fact I had another day. I practiced gratitude in all kinds of forms. I tried to fill the day with experiences to infuse my perspective with positive things. I didn't ignore God in it. I knew he would be the source of encouragement. After all, he is the source of everything, and he wants us to go to him for what we need.

I started the day reading my Bible and praying. I reflected and journaled on how God was with me, creating a record of how he was walking with me in the journey. I started listing the ways in which I saw God show up. Verses would jump off the page of my Bible, like someone was throwing them at me—words of encouragement spoken to the exact worry on my mind. Other times songs would play and pierce my heart with the message of God's incredible love, bringing hope into the room. I read stories of how God brought people through their own cancer journey, and I knew Jesus was using those stories to give me encouragement.

Then there was the mail. Good old snail mail. Many times, an encouraging note arrived in the mail, astonishing me with the timing. God had to prompt someone to write me a note, then mail it, then have it arrive on the exact day I was struggling. This happened over and over. What made this so astounding was the pandemic was playing absolute havoc with the mail. Staff shortages meant things were not running smoothly with the mail service. Something that should arrive within a day or two didn't come for weeks. Everyone was suddenly shopping for everything online, and the system was overwhelmed. You couldn't count on something arriving when it was supposed to. Within all the mess, God chose to coordinate and intervene to ensure words of encouragement arrived precisely when I needed them. When I opened a note and found beautiful life-giving words of encouragement, I often wept with the generosity of God. My heart would also be full of gratitude for the obedience of someone to respond to God's guiding and reach out to me. In a time where Covid kept me from connecting in person with people, these notes were like having a little piece of the person show up.

When I reflect on all the ways God showed up, I'm embarrassed to say for several months discouragement was still a daily battle. You see, as much as God was showing up, the enemy was also showing up. I would have a very good day, spent with all kinds of encouragement and positive experiences. As I was resting in that positive headspace, a horrible dark thought would pop into my mind. Or I would have a weird pain in my head, which would send me into worry. I couldn't escape the reality I was fighting cancer; my brain had been cut into, and the odds were stacked against me. The enemy used those realities to create uncertainty, fear, and discouragement. My life was never going to be the same. I was a cancer patient, and this reality now defined my life. Something had been taken from me. The optimism I used to approach life with was gone. I felt confident God was with me, but

I feared the places He was taking me. And I was getting very tired of the struggle.

"Do not be afraid or discouraged, for the Lord will personally go ahead of you. He will be with you; he will neither fail you nor abandon you." (Deuteronomy 31:8, NLT) This passage is often quoted when people are going through a hard time. It comes out of a story in the Old Testament where Moses is giving a charge to Joshua. The people of Israel had followed Moses as their leader. They had been on a forty-year journey culminating in crossing over the Jordan River and taking the land God promised to them. Moses had been the leader for the journey, but he would not finish with them. The task was given to Joshua. What a job. There would have been enough uncertainty for everyone to be overwhelmed by it. The people of Israel were about to enter a land with strong opposition against them, their leader would not be going with them, and the job was being given to someone without a lot of experience. The natural response to those circumstances would be fear and discouragement. How were they ever going to be successful? How would they stay alive?

Moses knew all of this. He had spent time with God, heard firsthand he would not be entering the land. He could have been resentful at the harshness of the punishment for his disobedience. But Moses' love for the people brought him to give specific instructions and encouragement, both to the people, and specifically to Joshua. "Be strong and of good courage, do not fear nor be afraid of them; for the Lord your God, He is the One who goes with you. He will not leave you nor forsake you" (Deuteronomy 31:6, NKJV). Moses addressed the fear of the people. He knew what they felt and spoke words of encouragement. He reminded them they are not going on their own. God would always be with them and never leave them. It wasn't the presence of Moses giving the people victory, but the presence of God.

Then Moses turned specifically to Joshua. He didn't take Joshua aside and give him a pep talk but an empowering charge, witnessed by the entire nation of Israel. This would be a moment Joshua could go back to when his confidence wavered. Others could remind him of Moses's charge when the days were exhausting and long. It was a moment of grounding, anchoring Joshua for the work ahead of him.

"Then Moses called Joshua and said to him in the sight of all Israel, 'Be strong and of good courage, for you must go with this people to the land which the LORD has sworn to their fathers to give them, and you shall cause them to inherit it. And the LORD, He is the one who goes before you. He will be with you, He will not leave you nor forsake you; do not fear nor be dismayed'" (Deuteronomy 31:7–8, NKJV). The instructions to Joshua have some similarity to the ones given to the people, such as the command at the beginning to be strong and of good courage. Both have the comfort of the promise God will never leave or forsake his people or Joshua. That's pretty powerful stuff. The presence of the Almighty will remain with Joshua and the people of Israel. This is why they can be confident enough to not be afraid when the circumstances would tell them to run.

While the two instructions from Moses are similar, the one to Joshua includes an interesting piece. "And the LORD, He is the one who goes before you." Before us, eh? That's interesting. It's an oft-quoted piece of Scripture, but what does it really mean? It's one I struggled with mightily. After all, if God goes before me, then he knew what was coming. He was there when the mistakes were being made leading to the misdiagnosis of the lump in my armpit, the origin of the cancer. That's hard to deal with. Why didn't he step in and correct the mistake, nudge the technician to take another sample? He knew what was coming, and he still pushed me to go through all the preparation for the new job. Why bother with all of it when I wasn't going to be well enough to do the job? If God goes before me, what's the point of him doing that? I kept coming around and around to that, like being on a bad ride at the fair that just spins round and round, going nowhere and leaving you feeling sick. Then one day, a friend showed up and stopped the ride, helped me climb off and find the grounding I was desperate for.

In the late days of fall, the weather was turning cooler, and winter lurked just around the corner. I'm not a fan of the cold, and my daily walks reminded me that soon the days would be short, dark, and frosty. It reflected my mood. I faced a long winter at home, mainly by myself, trying to fill the days and build my strength. The visits with people that had been such a source of energy were becoming a challenge. Covid meant visits should take place outside, and the cold was hindering these. I was in the middle of my immunotherapy treatments, and the side effects had subsided a bit. The fatigue was still huge, but I had lots of time to rest and manage my energy.

One day a friend called and wanted to come for a visit. I was looking forward to it. For someone who was used to spending the entire day interacting with people at work, day after day by myself was difficult. When my friend arrived, we decided to have a visit distanced inside. As we sat on opposite sides of the room, I could see something was up. She appeared nervous. I wondered if she was uncomfortable with the inside visit. She and her husband had graciously "bubbled up" with us during the height of the pandemic. This meant they restricted their contacts with people to a very few, including us in the list so we could maintain contact. It was a beautiful gesture of love and their care had been very sustaining. As we chit chatted about what life was like for each of us at the moment, she shifted on the couch. Something was clearly weighing on her. It wasn't long before she got to the heart of the matter. She had something she needed to share with me, and she wasn't sure how I would react. She had been praying, asking God if she could share it with me for months, but God had only released her to share now. The story she told rolled into the room and completely filled the space.

In January of 2020, she had been sitting in church as usual on a Sunday morning. Keith and I had been sitting with her and her husband. At the service I wasn't aware of what was going on, but God spoke directly to her during the prayer time. He told her she needed to get praying for someone. He told her this person had cancer in the area of her chest, that she was at the service, and she was going to need a lot of prayer. As the service ended, she looked around, wondering who the Lord was talking about. She went to another woman in the congregation, and asked if there was anyone who fit the description. Neither one of them could figure out who it was.

She knew she had to get praying, so she contacted a couple of her prayer partners. She explained what happened and asked them to join her in this prayer journey. Those three women began to pray. They didn't know who they were praying for, just the few details God had given.

A woman had cancer in the area of her chest, and they needed to be praying for this person. Every week, as they met to pray, they lifted up this woman God had laid on my friend's heart. They asked God to work, to heal, to encourage, to strengthen. Often, my friend asked God who it was, but that information was never revealed to her. She just kept praying.

Three months later, I landed in the hospital with a brain tumor. My friend and her husband supported us in so many ways. I knew they were praying for us, and this was a huge support. As I recuperated from the craniotomy, they stopped by for brief visits, brought food, and assured us of continued prayer. When the devastating diagnosis came, I shared the details with her. That's when she knew. Suddenly it was revealed who had been the object of her prayers. It was me! My original tumor was in my armpit, right beside my chest. I had been sitting right beside her that day in church. I had no symptoms and felt totally healthy. I was completely oblivious to the fact cancer was marching through my body. But God knew every single detail. He knew what was coming, and the huge battle it would be. For months before I had any idea what was going on in my body, God arranged for three women to pray for me. They stored up months of prayers on behalf of someone. They prayed weekly, faithfully.

As the story spilled out of my friend, I could hardly breathe. My heart began to beat harder with every sentence she spoke. My mind was racing to process. She had no clue what was happening to my body, I didn't even know. When I landed in the hospital, it was for a brain tumor. She added me to her prayer list, but also kept praying for the unnamed person God had told her about that January morning. Every week she and her prayer partners had been lifting me up to God. I was struck by their faithful obedience. It couldn't have been easy to persevere. After all, they didn't have any connection to the person they were praying for, not even a name. Still, they prayed. They had loved Jesus enough to believe if he asked them to do something without giving all the details, it was important to do, and they obeyed.

But it wasn't just the obedience of these women that struck me. As my friend talked, the love of Jesus just filled the room. All distractions were removed as a palpable presence invaded. All my focus was trained on this amazing story. My questions about what God was up to began to shrink. He had been up to something for months. When I was busy living my life, working at the new job, dealing with all of the day-to-day stuff, God was going ahead of me into the approaching battle. He was storing up strength through the prayers of these women. He knew every detail of the approaching storm and put provision for it in place for months before it arrived. God had gone before me in a powerful way. To realize this soaked me with the love of God to the core. Any doubts were washed away in that wave of love. If God was going to such lengths to provide for me, to go before me, then I was in good hands. The need to know why shrunk.

For months, my friend had been asking God if it was okay to share this story with me. She and her prayer partners were still praying for me, by name now. Finally, she felt God release her to share, and that day in the late fall, her story became my powerful message from God. He was totally in control. He wasn't in the background watching what was happening to me. He was ahead of me, preparing powerful strength to get me through the battle.

For reasons I don't think I will know this side of heaven, God has allowed the storm of serious cancer into my life. When the complicated and heavy things are allowed into our lives, when God doesn't prevent the storms, it's so hard. I had agonized over the "why" of it all. What I've learned is that why is not always ours to know. God's greater purpose and plan isn't always evident to our human understanding. The story God is writing with our lives doesn't have the final chapter revealed until we get to heaven. In the meantime, we have to keep living our stories.

When I was in university, there was a particular art form that became popular, autostereograms. The artist would create a picture, but at first glance it looked only like a bunch of repeating colors and shapes. If you looked at the individual pieces, the picture was pleasing, but you couldn't take in the whole image. In order to see the intended image, you had to stand back and allow your eyes to become unfocused on the specifics of the picture. Once you did this, a three-dimensional image would appear. It was surprising. Focusing on the details never allowed you to see what the artist had hidden there. Only when you stepped back and stopped trying to control what you were seeing did a very clear picture appear.

I think our lives are like this. God is creating something with each of our stories. The details are closest to us, and that's what we get focused on. Everything we experience, the great, the horrible, and everything in between, adds a piece to the image. We have a hard time seeing the overall image. Stepping back isn't easy. We have to relax, let go of trying to figure it out, and allow the Spirit of God to direct our vision. That day, as my friend shared her story with me, God helped me step back and get a glimpse of the image he is creating with my life. There is so much more there than I understand if I only focus on the details.

Stepping back, I saw almighty God, the creator of everything, the source of all strength and power, creating provision for me. He initiated a process of storing up prayers for me. He went before me, and I didn't have any idea what he was doing. He was in my cancer journey before I knew there was a cancer journey coming. If God will go to those lengths, take the time to speak to someone else to intercede for me, to put the process in motion before I am aware of the need, then maybe I can trust him with the question of why and not need an answer. God didn't prevent this storm, but he showed up in every minute of it. His purpose will one day be revealed.

In that moment I caught a brief glimpse of the image God is creating with my life. It is an image pointing to him, reflecting his magnificent glory and power and strength. God really does go before us. We are so often unaware of how he is working. Maybe we miss it sometimes. Getting trapped in the circumstances of the moment narrows our vision. In those times, it takes a very purposeful act of our will to step back, to stop focusing on the immediate circumstances. But if we do, if we allow ourselves to let our vision be controlled by God's Spirit, we can catch a glimpse of the beautiful picture God is creating with our lives. We were meant to reflect God, his glory, his power, his love.

In my living room that afternoon, as I stepped back and allowed God to focus my vision, what I saw was love. The love of a God who would get things prepared for me before I knew I needed them. A God who loved me so much he got others involved in the process. A God who was so intimately involved in all the details. While I had gotten caught up in the circumstances, God was lovingly creating a picture that would bring the focus onto him, his power, his strength, his love.

This is why he said to not be afraid or discouraged. When God is willing to go to those lengths for me, how could I be discouraged? At that moment, I was no longer seeing my life through the water of discouragement. God reached down and pulled the picture of my life out of the water. As the discouragement poured off and dripped away, I was able to focus clearly. I saw the beauty of Jesus. The love of Jesus was radiating from every piece. I was completely loved, cared for, and Jesus was with me. In that picture, the need to know why faded into the background.

We all struggle with the why of circumstances at some point in our lives. The job that provides for us ends suddenly in layoff. Why? Our child is relentlessly bullied at school. Why? The friend we confided in betrays our trust. Why? The spouse chooses to leave. Why? Death rips our cherished one away from us. Why? It's human to ask the question. It's especially human to ask the question of God. After all, he is all knowing, and all loving. Where is his love in the midst of the shattering pain? I can't answer your question of why. It's not my place to try. But I can tell you this. When you take your question and direct it to Jesus, he hears you.

The Father knows the grief and ache in your heart. The Spirit gathers the pain that causes tears to flood your being. Jesus intimately understands us and wants to walk with us in these journeys. He doesn't barge in where he isn't welcome, but it only takes a small turn towards him to see he is right there. We are not promised a pass on life's pain and heartaches, but we are promised a whole lot. We are promised the presence of God in every minute, the provision of God in every step, and the love of God that means we never face a circumstance alone. You have no idea how God is working in your circumstances right now, this very minute. You may not be aware of what is ahead, but God is, and he is already there working for your good.

Giving your question of why to Jesus, surrendering it to him and leaving it with him, is a huge step. I get it. There were many days of tough slogging, the question of why weighing me down, holding me from moving forward like an anchor. I am full of thankfulness. Jesus took my questions of why and answered by allowing me to see a clearer picture of what he is creating with my life. When that picture begins to get fuzzy around the edges, I think back to the story my friend told me. I meditate on the message of provision God shone into my life. I remember that God went before me and powerfully provided for me. Will He do it again? That's what I'm counting on!

I will be still and know that you are God.

You are my refuge and strength, an ever-present help in trouble. Therefore, I will not fear.

But as for me, I will always have hope; I will praise you more and more.

I praise you Lord for being my guide. Even in the darkest night, your teachings fill my mind. I will keep my eyes always on the Lord. With him at my right hand, I will not be shaken. Therefore, my heart is glad, and my tongue rejoices, and my body will also rest secure.

Though you have made me see troubles, many and bitter, you will restore my life again, from the depths of the earth you will again bring me up.

Lord, in all the challenges that lie ahead, help me to trust in you. My times are in your hands ... Let your face shine on your servant; save me in your unfailing love. Let me not be put to shame Lord, for I have cried out to you.

Help me to give my entire attention to what you are doing right now, and not get worked up about what may or may not happen tomorrow. I claim the promise that God will help me deal with whatever hard things come up when the time comes.

Give me faith to not be afraid or discouraged for I believe the Lord will personally go ahead of me. He will be with me. He will neither fail me nor abandon me.

Chapter 9

Spread your protection over them ...
Cover him with favor as with a shield.
Psalm 5:11–12 ESV

S hopping. We all do it. Somehow those products end up in our possession, whether it's food, a chair, or a part for the broken lawn mower. We all shop for things. How do you shop? Do you wander around the store, taking in all the products until you find something that appeals to you? Or do you have a goal, looking only in the areas of the store that will have what you want? Maybe your shopping is all online, but the same principle applies. Do you meander around the online platform, or are you focused on finding just the item on your list?

I tend to be more of a goal-oriented person, and this usually applies to my shopping. I don't leave to buy groceries without a list. I plan which stores I will shop at, choosing certain stores based on what I need on any particular list. My husband has similar tendencies. It doesn't mean we don't get sucked into impulse buys or that our sons haven't talked us into things over the years, but we regularly get in and out of a store with only the items on our list.

However, we each have our exceptions. For me, it's the mall. I grew up in the era of going to the mall to shop. Having so many stores in one location was genius to my way of thinking. As a teen, spending a Saturday at the mall was an event. My friends and I would plan for days ahead, talking endlessly about what we would shop for. We were the annoying group that probably talked a little too loudly, while touching everything in the store. I'm sure store clerks moaned silently as they watched their neatly folded piles disappear in our wake. So even now, when I enter a mall something comes over me, and my goal-oriented shopping mind takes a back seat. I wander, I window shop, I browse, I snack; it's an event. The reason I came to the mall takes a back seat to the experience.

My husband comes up against the same thing when he goes to his favorite parts store. All manner of equipment lines the shelves, from supplies needed for auto repair, home renovations, and camping, to a huge variety of surplus items. The first time he went to that store, he came home so excited. I tried to follow as he explained the huge variety of amazing items with great animation. He couldn't wait to show me. So, the next time he took me with him. We wandered around every inch of the store. I had no clue what half the items were, so he patiently explained the purpose of the items to me. We walked slowly and deliberately. He didn't want to miss a thing on the loaded shelves. It was an experience. Even to this day he will go to get a specific item and come home with numerous treasures in the back of the truck. This change in our approach to shopping, whether it be a mall or parts store, was about our perspective. Our focus was on being there, in that particular building, willingly taking in all that was offered in the experience.

In so many ways, God took my focus during my cancer journey and changed what I was looking at. He slowed me down, forced me to take in everything in my surroundings, and he even patiently talked to me and guided me. After the revelation my friend's story brought, the healing of my emotions gave me space to consider what I would do with my time. Up until that point, I had been existing, focusing on the next physical challenge, checking things off an imagined cancer to-do list.

Now, I began to consider what I would do with my days in a whole new light. I had been blessed with tremendous healing in my spirit, and God began talking with me about what I would do with that gift. I started to explore what options I had. I prayed God would lead me to something where I could minister and help people. Being in a pandemic, it wasn't like I could just go out and volunteer at some organization. Almost everything was virtual. The usual avenues to be involved at church were on hold. I reached out to a couple of organizations that had some virtual opportunities. The process was slow, and nothing really seemed like a good fit. I kept praying. I had whole days where there wasn't anything on my to-do list, and they were long. My energy steadily increased, and I felt like I could handle doing something with purpose. I really wanted to help someone like I had been helped. I had been on the receiving end of so much, and I wanted to give back. But how?

In praying, God quieted my heart. As I spent more and more time reading my Bible, I found evidence of God answering prayers with amazing timing. I began to ask God for a fresh set of eyes to see whatever need was there. Instead of praying for direction to a specific ministry, I asked God to show me the needs around me. One day, as I was reading some online communication from a relative, I thought to myself, "*Wow, she is really discouraged.*" Then God asked me a clear question. "How can you encourage her?" I wanted to help and thought I could send her a message. But that didn't seem to be enough.

Online communication is often fleeting in both the sending and receiving. As I pondered how I could encourage her, God brought to mind all the ways people encouraged me. One of the most impactful were the notes I received in the mail. Someone taking the time to send a written message really encouraged me. I kept the notes as physical reminders and pulled them out on hard days. I was also touched by the extra effort put into sending a physical note.

I remembered the letter I had received from an aunt. She was also in the middle of a cancer journey, and she sent me a letter with some note cards inside. On the notecards she had attached a mustard seed and the verses from Matthew 17 that talk about faith as small as a mustard seed having the strength to move a mountain. Reading that verse, I couldn't take my eyes off the mustard seed. It was just so small. It didn't have the appearance of anything significant, anything that could amount to much. Such a small seed had enormous potential, and I realized my faith also had enormous potential. The seed of faith, planted in the soil of God's word, and watered with prayer would yield big things. That message of encouragement revived my resolve to lean in more to Jesus. As I reflected on this gift of encouragement, it became clear to me. I needed to get writing. I searched through my desk and found some note cards. I even found a few stamps. Guess I had the materials I needed.

As I opened a card to begin writing, I stared at the blank space. Questions started to sprout. What should I say? How could I possibly encourage someone who was going through so much? Would the words be taken the right way? What if something was misinterpreted? Doubt started to creep in. Before the doubt could get firmly rooted, I began to pray. I asked Jesus to give me the right words that would be an encouragement. I kept praying until I felt at peace, and then I began to write.

The words came. As I finished and read over what I had written, I knew it wasn't me. Jesus wrote that card. I could sense his presence in the words. That evening I shared the note with my husband, asking for his input. His positive response confirmed I was on the right track. The next day I addressed the note, prayed over it, and mailed it off. As I walked back from the mailbox, I realized I had found my thing, my way to give back and encourage people. I would write and send notes of encouragement.

I started asking God to show me who needed encouragement. As I prayed this every day, different people would come to mind. I spent time in prayer before I ever penned a word. Sometimes a Bible verse would come to mind, and I would include it. Most of the cards were written in draft form first, then I would pray about what I had written. Sometimes the focus of the card ended up being quite different than what I started out with. I surrendered each one to Jesus, asking him to use the words to bring the kind of encouragement only Jesus can bring.

"Spread your protection over them ... cover him with favour as with a shield." (Psalm 5:11–12 ESV) Asking for protection from God was something I had been taught as a child. Every night as I was tucked into bed, my parents guided me through prayers that asked for protection. Before heading out on trips, we prayed, asking for protection. I had held others up to God in a whole variety of circumstances, asking him to protect them. Now, in a cancer battle, the prayer for protection had a deeper nuance. My resources weren't enough, and I had to rely on God's protection on an emotional level, not just the physical. I needed protection from the dark emotional traps waiting for me, ready to spring.

Attacks came unexpectedly. Battles in the mind could become intense quickly. I needed to pray daily for protection. These portions from Psalm 5 had become part of my daily prayers for months. I used them when I was going into appointments to bring calm. I recited them over and over as I lay in the scans. During the sleepless hours in the middle of the night, they became my plea. These words had brought me so much peace and encouragement. I believed God poured out protection and favor over every facet of my life. Now God was showing me that the words he had given me in these verses weren't just for me. He was ready and waiting to pour out his protection and favor over others. It was my job to pray that for them, to encourage them like I had been encouraged. I had been blessed with so much protection and favor, and I needed to share with others. Those promises needed to be claimed by others too, and my words of encouragement could guide them to the blessings.

Shields were a well-known piece of equipment for soldiers in biblical times. Being covered with a shield meant significant protection for a soldier. In Ephesians 6, Paul uses the analogy of a shield to describe a person's faith.[4] The Roman shield he referenced was meant to cover the body, giving full protection. A Roman shield would have animal hide in its construction, so it needed regular oiling to keep it soft, pliable, and useful. Proper care and regular attention would mean the shield could function as protection when needed. The soldier still wore armor on his body, but the shield added an extra layer against powerful weapons used in battle.

Asking God to cover us like a shield is a request for full protection, an extra layer when the battle is tough and feels overwhelming. To keep protection ready and near, we need to give attention to God and search his Word for instructions, so we are ready for him to use. This is the process of growing our faith. When our thoughts are weighed down by doubt, fear, and uncertainty, we can't hear him as clearly as we should, and the protection isn't as pliable as it should be. The arrows of the enemy can slip through in those times.

It might seem counterintuitive to our human logic, but one of the ways God strengthens us is through giving to others, ministering to their needs. Second Corinthians talks about extending ourselves through giving to others. "Yes, God is more than ready to overwhelm you with every form of grace, so that you will have more than enough of everything —every moment and in every way. He will make you overflow with abundance in every good thing you do." (2 Corinthians 9:8, TPT) God had indeed extended his grace to me in all forms. He was enough for me in every moment and in every way. Now it was time to take his abundance and share it, pour it into other people's lives and allow it to flow. God had been pouring abundantly into my life through my whole cancer journey. I had learned deep and powerful lessons. I had grown to trust him in ways I didn't know were possible. Now it was time to share the overflow.

After the initial note, it didn't take long for God to guide me to a new person to write to. As I followed the prayerful writing task, I knew it was God writing those notes. It wasn't always easy. Sometimes he asked me to write to people who I had some history with, people who weren't my favorite. He stretched me in those requests. The focus was not on myself. It had to be on the other person. As God continued to lead, I realized he was changing my focus. It wasn't a goal-oriented task, where I had to get a note written. It was about allowing God to direct me to be more observant of those around me. To take the time and see everything around me, meander through life and the circumstances others were experiencing. It wasn't about getting something done, it was about the experience of encouraging others, and the process involved in that.

My awareness of the needs around me grew. God took me to the store of his encouragement, and had me wander around the aisles slowly, carefully taking in the people lining the shelves. It was an experience. As we browsed that store, he would point out someone specific, the need for encouragement, and when I took them off the shelf, I knew he would give me what I needed to encourage them. At the checkout, it was Jesus who paid the bill. His love poured out on the cross covered everything that was owed. I was merely the conduit for his love, the one who took the time to see the need and ask Jesus to meet it. What a privilege and a blessing to be part of that work.

That's the incredible thing about walking with Jesus. He takes something and uses it for so many purposes. The notes I wrote were intended to encourage others, to take Jesus' love and pour it over their lives. God didn't stop there though. As he took me through the process, I grew. It was such a blessed opportunity to be part of encouraging others. I didn't always know how God used the notes, but there were times he allowed me to see how he had taken the notes and used them to help someone. The creativity of God always astounded me in those moments. That's the thing about God. He works in ways we don't always understand, yet it is always for his good purposes. I don't know why God allowed my cancer, but in the healing process, I was able to take the lessons I had learned and share them with others. God used the suffering to help someone else. He didn't leave me; he extended his grace to someone else through me. What an incredible God!

This whole journey of note writing taught me something. I need to slow down, to browse the aisles of God's store, because laying there on the shelves are blessings I will miss if my focus is too narrow, and my speed is too quick. God taught me to slow down, that it's ok to meander because he is always there. His timing is impeccable; his grace is bountiful. In our meandering with God, we quiet down enough to allow him to fine tune our perspective. Our minds begin to hear him more clearly. We can discern the details of his purposes. I am still awestruck God would partner with me to fulfill his purposes. I guess that comes with the position of being a daughter to the King. That's pretty powerful stuff.

God really doesn't need me to get things done. Yet he wants me to partner with him and spread his love. The Holy Spirit who raised Jesus back to life lives in me. That's huge! The power that is available to me is the same power now living in me in the form of the Holy Spirit. All of this has made me bolder. I come to Jesus now with more faith and more trust. I'm also making some big requests. I have people who are in my circle who don't walk with Jesus. I ask God to show me how to share him with them in new ways. I pray they see and hear Jesus instead of seeing and hearing me.

Every day I pray Jesus would fill my mind with thoughts from him, so I can discern what I should say and do. I don't always get it right. Sometimes the goal-oriented part of me takes over and I forge ahead in order to get something done. I make my own list instead of browsing God's shelves. I decide ahead of time what should happen and how it should happen. That's when things don't turn out exactly right. I don't end up with what I should have at the checkout, and this hinders the work of God. Thankfully, God is incredibly patient with me. He allows me to go back to the shelves and find what he wants me to focus on. He gently redirects me and puts my perspective back into the proper focus, so once again I can continue his way. He faithfully proves himself enough.

I will be still and know that you are God.

You are my refuge and strength, an ever-present help in trouble. Therefore, I will not fear.

But as for me, I will always have hope; I will praise you more and more.

I praise you, Lord, for being my guide. Even in the darkest night, your teachings fill my mind. I will keep my eyes always on the Lord. With him at my right hand, I will not be shaken. Therefore, my heart is glad, and my tongue rejoices, and my body will also rest secure.

Though you have made me see troubles, many and bitter, you will restore my life again, from the depths of the earth you will again bring me up.

Lord, in all the challenges that lie ahead, help me to trust in you. My times are in your hands ... Let your face shine on your servant; save me in your unfailing love. Let me not be put to shame, Lord, for I have cried out to you.

Help me to give my entire attention to what you are doing right now, and not get worked up about what may or may not happen tomorrow. I claim the promise that God will help me deal with whatever hard things come up when the time comes.

Give me faith to not be afraid or discouraged for I believe the Lord will personally go ahead of me. He will be with me. He will neither fail me nor abandon me.

Oh God, spread your protection over me. Father, cover me with favor as with a shield.

Chapter 10

So we're not giving up. How could we!
Even though on the outside it often looks
like things are falling apart on us, on the
inside, where God is making new life, not
a day goes by without his unfolding grace.
2 Corinthians 4:16–18, MSG

How's your eyesight? It can be something we take for granted, until it doesn't work like it should. Just before I turned fifty, I noticed I was having difficulty with small print. I needed to stretch my arm out a little longer to read the fine print on labels. Then the print in some books began to get a little fuzzy. Reading, an activity I always loved, began to be frustrating, even causing a headache sometimes. So, I did the only reasonable thing I could think of. I stopped reading small print. I carefully selected books that had larger print, zoomed up the text size on devices, and carried on.

Then it came time for an eye checkup. My eyes had always been 20/20, and I assumed that would continue. I remember the optometrist smiling when he told me I needed reading glasses. He asked if I had noticed any changes, and as I described how I had been changing my reading habits, a light flicked on. There had been changes going on, and I didn't bother to recognize what was happening. My sight was changing, but I didn't slow down or pause to consider what was going on. I had made adjustments without reflecting on why I needed them and just carried on. Once I got the glasses and began to use them, the difference was stark. I didn't avoid text that was too small. I could read whatever I wanted to again.

Many times during my cancer journey, my focus was a little blurry. There were times when I felt like I could hardly see. The road ahead just seemed to end in a fuzzy space of uncertainty. Much of the journey was character-ized by "hurry up and wait." The doctor would determine what the problem was, what treatment was needed, and then I would just have to wait. Wait for appointments, wait for results, wait for medication to work. Just so much waiting! And in waiting, it was hard to figure out where I should focus.

Now don't get me wrong. I knew I should focus on Jesus. I knew he was with me. But sometimes we can get out of focus and not even realize it. We look for the easy thing, the quick remedy to our issue. Just like how I changed to larger text when my eyesight got worse, the easy thing was always closer. It was easier to get all caught up in the doom and gloom of the prognosis for my disease. After all, these were medical doctors and researchers who had studied my cancer. They knew what they were talking about. Accepting what they said was logical. Looking to God, and his possibilities required me to open my eyes wide. To take the focus off the human realm and plant it firmly with Jesus. "What if ..." was always one of Satan's biggest attacks. He would sneak it in every chance he got. The next appointment, test, or treatment was easily clouded with "what if." It would keep gloom around the edges, not allowing me to see clearly.

The revelation that came with my friend's story changed my perspective. I began to view "what if" differently. Before that revelation, after the "what if" came *What if you die, what if your brain is impaired, what if you can't go back to work.* Now my sight had been changed, the perspective rearranged. The new narrative sounded like this: *What if your strength returns, what if your sons see you trusting Jesus, what if God uses this for something positive, what if he extends your life.* I began to believe for a future. The days started to have a purpose beyond just surviving. I could thrive in this cancer journey.

"So we're not giving up. How could we! Even though on the outside it often looks like things are falling apart on us, on the inside, where God is making new life, not a day goes by without His unfolding grace" (2 Cor. 4:16–18, MSG). These words were written by someone who knew about pain and suffering. The author, Paul, was writing to a group of people who knew him as he had started the church in Corinth. This is a rather personal letter. Paul is writing to those who know him well. He has been through a tremendous amount of suffering: brutal whippings and beatings, a shipwreck where he spent a day adrift in the sea, hunger, lack of proper protection against cold, people actively trying to stop his ministry. No wonder he says the outside looks like things are falling apart. Anyone observing his life would wonder why he continued instead of giving up.

For all the suffering Paul knew, he also had learned about overcoming. He doesn't boast about beating the odds or toughing things out. His reason for continuing is grounded in his relationship with Jesus, and his belief that Jesus can use suffering to grow faith and bring glory to God.

To someone on the outside, my circumstances looked dire. Indeed, I often received those looks of pity people give someone who is going through tough circumstances. You know the look. One that has compassion, but behind the eyes is a pity because they don't believe anything will get better. I never blamed anyone for that look. My circumstances were bleak to outsiders. It really did look like things were falling apart. I had learned the power of Jesus' constant, continual presence meant that it didn't feel bleak on the inside. There truly was a new life being created within me, sustaining me.

People would sometimes remark they didn't know how I was managing everything, and I had to agree with them. I really didn't understand how I was managing it either. Jesus was doing the work, the hard work of creating something positive out of horrible circumstances. Every single day, Jesus was pouring his grace into me, covering my life with his peace and strength. God gave me a glimpse of how far I had come in the cancer battle, and how strong in Christ I was. He had something for me in this, and there really can be treasure found in darkness.

I had begun to discern how to help others through my letter writing. I discovered there was more to that. Sharing my story encouraged people. I had several opportunities to share my testimony with people in different venues. Each time, God spoke to people, encouraging them in their own struggles. I was amazed at how God could use my simple story.

I neared the end of my year of treatment. I had been feeling very strong physically, and the doctor had allowed me to return to work virtually part time. It felt so good to be doing something "normal." There was a period of adjustment as my brain and body adapted to the cognitive demand of virtual work, but my strength grew. I was able to increase the length of the days, and after a couple of

to watch the pain, fear, and sadness wash over those you love. I even considered keeping the news to myself for a moment. I now understood why some make that decision. I had learned trying to go it alone would lead to an isolation that would take me to dark places. I had never held back from my family and friends. I had leaned on them, invited them into the journey, and they had been a tremendous network of support and care. So, I made the decision to share the news of the recurrence.

Once more we were forced through the "hurry up and wait" for more tests and results. It took six weeks to schedule all the scans. Six long weeks of waiting. In the months previous, I had agreed to record a podcast with a friend, and we were scheduled to make the recording that month. She was pastoring a church and doing weekly podcasts as part of her ministry. Now, with the recurrence I felt like I just couldn't do it. I didn't have the emotional space or strength to talk about my cancer journey. Everything was raw and too exposed. I told the Lord it wasn't going to happen. Everyone would understand. I had the perfect excuse. Despite all my excellent reasons, God still wouldn't let me off the hook. I knew I needed to go ahead and make the recording. As I prepared, I prayed really hard. This was beyond me, and I knew it had to be done in the Lord's strength because I didn't have an ounce of strength left.

I was reminded again of the verses in 2 Corinthians 4, "So we're not giving up. How could we! Even though on the outside it often looks like things are falling apart on us, on the inside, where God is making new life, not a day goes by without His unfolding grace." I didn't want to give up. I had seen God move in my life. I had experienced his presence profoundly. I knew he was in every moment. The outward circumstances looked like things were falling apart, but I knew Jesus could be enough for those moments. I had to allow him to be my strength. So, I leaned in hard, so very, very hard to Jesus. I don't really understand how, but Jesus gave me the words and prepared me to share. As we made that podcast recording, I knew it wasn't me speaking; it wasn't my words. God himself spoke that night. He was complete strength in my utter weakness. At the end of the podcast my friend asked me how I was doing, and I shared the cancer had returned. She prayed for me, and it was a very precious time.

I was totally unprepared for what happened next. I had thought the podcast was just for her church members, but it turns out she had a lot more followers than I realized. The podcast went out, and suddenly I began to get messages. People from all over, people I had never met, watched the podcast and started praying for me. They sent me messages of encouragement and assured me of their prayers. What a boost at a time when I was so uncertain. God asked me to do something. I didn't think I could do it. I told him that. He pressed me to go ahead, and when I did, he used the recording to give me a wealth of encouragement and prayer support I didn't know was possible. It sustained me through those long days of waiting.

Six weeks passed. It was time for the next appointment. As Keith and I waited for the doctor to walk through the door, I contemplated everything the last two years had brought. I didn't know what was ahead, but I knew one thing with utter certainty. Jesus was with me, had never left me, and he was already there in whatever was coming. I was his and that was enough. His presence in my life was enough.

The doctor walked in and began to go through the results of the tests and scans. She was stumbling around with her words a bit, and didn't seem her usual confident, composed self. Then she just paused. When she looked up at us, her tone registered disbelief. "I don't know how to say this, but I was wrong. Your cancer is not back. The mass in your brain is still there but it doesn't have any blood flowing to it. The spot on your lung has completely disappeared. There isn't any indication of cancer in your body anywhere. As of right now, we consider you cancer free."

Jesus had miraculously healed me! My doctor was in disbelief. She didn't know what to say. I could see the confusion and disbelief on her face underneath her smile. I looked at Keith. We both had huge smiles of relief. We hugged and even shed some tears. We knew what had happened. Jesus had intervened.

I have spent a lot of time reflecting on that news, the healing I received. I've had to process it like every other piece of this journey. Sometimes the devil continues to be up to his usual habits and throws doubt on the healing. After all, didn't the doctor just say she made a mistake? I don't buy it though. It wasn't just one doctor who said the cancer was back. I had a couple of different scans. The techs who completed the scans and doctors who read those scans and wrote the reports all agreed there was recurrence. When a group of medical professionals agree, I tend to believe it. My oncologist didn't have a good explanation for that kind of mistake. Everyone in that group had to be mistaken, which seems illogical to me. But then, my explanation of things disappearing and blood flow stopping isn't very logical to their medical minds. I could go round and round in my mind, but that is a waste of time. What I know, and am certain of, is this: Jesus healed me.

Living in that space, the healing that came from Jesus has meant so many things. I have a story to tell. I feel responsible to ensure my story always points to Jesus. So many people have been involved in my story, prayed for me, and I need to let them know how God worked. I still don't understand why God allowed me to walk through this trial, but I know there are things for me here. I have learned to seek the treasure in the dark times.

What does all this mean for my future? Another question without a direct answer. That hasn't been revealed to me yet. In 2 Kings, chapter 6, we are told the story of Elisha. When you read the incredible ways God worked through him, it is awe inspiring. He did all kinds of things that defied explanation. In verses 14–17, the outward circumstances were grim. A great army had come in the night and surrounded Israel, Elisha, and all who were with him. Elisha's servant is understandably afraid. There may have even been panic and hopelessness in his voice as he asked Elisha, "Oh no, my lord! What shall we do?" (2 Kings 6:15, NIV)

This is someone who had seen miraculous and mighty acts performed by Elisha in the name of God. He should be feeling confident, but the outward circumstances are too negative to ignore. I love Elisha's response. He didn't berate his servant for unbelief. He spoke right to the heart of the matter, the fear. Elisha shared his perspective, what he saw. The perspective of these two men was so different. One was looking out at a powerful army ready to wipe out everyone in its path. The other was looking out at the provision God had placed over Israel. But the servant couldn't see the provision and needed God to open his eyes.

"Don't be afraid," the prophet answered. "Those who are with us are more than those who are with them." And Elisha prayed, "Open his eyes, Lord, so that he may see." (2 Kings 6:16-17, NIV) Elisha understood his servant's fear. It made human sense to be terrified when facing that kind of threat. His prayer was so kind. He wanted his servant to see what he saw, to have the confidence he had because of the army God had provided. He knew only seeing would give the explanation of what God was doing.

In giving me a miraculous physical healing, Jesus gave me a small glimpse of heaven. You see, every miracle has a message. This was a story needing to be told, shared, proclaimed. God was working and I couldn't recognize it. I didn't see the army of angels surrounding me, claiming my health for Jesus. But God opened my eyes and gave me his perspective to see he has a whole other purpose he is working out. "Don't be afraid!" Elisha told him. "For there are more on our side than on theirs!" (2 Kings 6:16, NLT) No matter what the circumstance, there are more on my side than I know. The miracles are real and still happening. They didn't stop with Elisha. They didn't stop with Jesus' ministry on earth. Miracles are still happening today. I know because I am one.

It was about six weeks after I returned to work in the same school I was working in when I got sick. It had been wonderful to return and reconnect with everyone. One day, my office administrator came and stood at my door. She had a reflective look on her face. After a few moments she spoke. "You're a miracle aren't you, Heather."

I smiled at her. "I have received an incredible miracle of healing." She smiled and walked back to her desk. I don't know the exact progression of her thoughts that led to that brief interaction, but I do know this. When confronted with proof of God at work, people will acknowledge miracles. When circumstances defy logical explanation, people do believe in miracles. Having received a tremendous miracle, I know I need to share it. I can't back down, let doubt creep in, or water down the truth.

I now face each day with the confidence that there are more on my side than on the other side. More than I can see, and more than I can imagine. Things looked so grim. The outward circumstances looked like they were falling apart. Jesus was enough for those circumstances. He came and worked a miracle in my body, gave healing, and not a day goes by without new life and his unfailing grace. He is enough!

I will be still and know that you are God.

You are my refuge and strength, an ever-present help in trouble. Therefore, I will not fear.

But as for me, I will always have hope; I will praise you more and more.

I praise you, Lord, for being my guide. Even in the darkest night, your teachings fill my mind. I will keep my eyes always on the Lord. With him at my right hand I will not be shaken. Therefore, my heart is glad, and my tongue rejoices, and my body will also rest secure.

Though you have made me see troubles, many and bitter, you will restore my life again, from the depths of the earth you will again bring me up.

Lord, in all the challenges that lie ahead, help me to trust in you. My times are in your hands ... Let your face shine on your servant; save me in your unfailing love. Let me not be put to shame Lord, for I have cried out to you.

Help me to give my entire attention to what you are doing right now and not get worked up about what may or may not happen tomorrow. I claim the promise that God will help me deal with whatever hard things come up when the time comes.

Give me faith to not be afraid or discouraged for I believe the Lord will personally go ahead of me. He will be with me. He will neither fail me nor abandon me.

Oh God, spread your protection over me. Father, cover me with favor as with a shield.

So we're not giving up. How could we! Even though on the outside it often looks like things are falling apart on us, on the inside, where God is making new life, not a day goes by without His unfolding grace.

Chapter 11

Now, because of you, Lord, I will lie down
in peace, and sleep comes at once, for no
matter what happens, I will live unafraid!
Psalm 4:8, TPT

Ahhh, sleep. I remember thinking when I was younger that sleep was optional. After all, there was so much to do, and so much to experience. I didn't want to miss anything! Then, as I had children, sleep became an elusive piece of life that was always in short supply, but I desperately longed for it. There was always just so much to do, and sleep was at the bottom of the list. I would get to it when all the other demands were met. This often left me living in a sleep-deprived state.

When stress arrived, heralded by some new circumstance, sleep became hard to find. It wasn't that I wasn't tired. When I lay down, I knew my body was ready to sleep, needed to sleep. But my mind would begin to replay the stress, the circumstance plaguing me, and it would take hours to get to sleep. When I came across this verse in Psalm 4, it was during a time when sleep was hard. The combination of medication and the circumstances of cancer had joined forces to keep me awake for hours.

I remember actually laughing when I first read the verse. *Sleep comes at once? That's impossible!*

Sleep has a specific purpose. Our bodies need it to recharge. Our brains need a chance to sort through the day and process. The immune system functions while we sleep, allowing our bodies to heal more efficiently. Adequate sleep allows our body and mind to function optimally. All of the restorative properties sleep was designed for are crucial. When stress comes and steals our ability to sleep, we feel the impact in all areas of our lives. I was certainly feeling that impact. At a point where my frustration levels were growing, I read this verse. I wanted to know how it was possible for sleep to come at once.

I went back and reread Psalm 4. It starts with David crying out to God. "Answer me when I call to you, my righteous God. Give me relief from my distress; have mercy on me and hear my prayer." (Psalm 4:1, NIV) You can hear the passion. This wasn't David just lifting words to heaven. He wanted God to give attention to his distress, and he was pleading for relief from slander and lies. As he outlines his grief and despair over the actions of those trying to ruin him, he turns to self-examination to calm himself before God. "Tremble and do not sin; when you are on your beds, search your hearts and be silent." (Psalm 4:4, NIV) David had justification for his anger, but he didn't want to let it become something that would separate him from God. His trust must remain rooted in God, both his experience of God in the past, and the belief God's ways are above man's. Focusing his thoughts this way, David can receive a blessing from God. "Now, because of you, Lord, I will lie down in peace, and sleep comes at once, for no matter what happens, I will live unafraid." (Psalm 4:8, TPT)

David affirms his trust in God, and in return comes a blessing of peace. This peace couldn't be taken away, because it was a gift from God. David had a choice to make. He could lie down and think about all the horrible things people were saying about him, or he could lie down and think about the trust he had in God. In determining his focus, he determined his level of peace. He had to deliberately release the circumstances in order to receive the peace. That's how God works. We can't grab hold of what God has for us if we don't let go of whatever is in our hands.

I started asking myself some hard questions. *What is keeping me up? What am I holding on to that keeps me from receiving peace?* Those were not easy questions. As they played over in my mind, I kept coming back to one word, trust. David had to trust completely God was going to come through for him. To be able to lie down in peace and sleep requires an acceptance of where we are and what is happening. *Oh God, I hate where I am! I don't want to be a cancer patient. This is all so out of my control.* And there it was. I needed to trust God was in control and let go of the fear and anxiety I clung to. I needed hands that were empty so I could grab on to the peace Jesus offered.

I don't know how long I have left on this earth. Even after receiving a "cancer free" proclamation from the doctor, I still struggle over the future. The medical community will only talk about the present, as there aren't any guarantees. If I focus on the statistics for my type of cancer, go down a Google rabbit hole, the uncertainty only grows. There is so much I don't know. Sometimes when I listen to people making plans, talking about the future, I begin to wonder about my own future. *Will I be around to meet my grandchildren? Will I even get to retirement?* I don't know. So how do I live unafraid?

"Now, because of you, Lord, I will lie down in peace, and sleep comes at once, for no matter what happens, I will live unafraid." (Psalm 4:8, TPT) David ends the Psalm with quite a declaration. *Live unafraid no matter what happens? How can that be? I'm looking at life and death here.* David was looking at life and death too. He had people actively wanting to kill him. How did he live unafraid? This is where looking at verses in context is so important. David wasn't making a flippant statement. The preceding verses are full of distress, his cries to God. Life was not easy, and circumstances were not fair. David went through a process of remembering what God had done for him, talking to God about the circumstances.

Through that he came to a place where he could receive a blessing of peace and confidence. He demonstrated a huge amount of trust in his declaration to live unafraid.

My expectations for life were getting in the way of allowing complete trust. *I want a long life! I want to be around to meet my grandchildren one day. Keith and I should be able to grow old together. I want to be able to retire and enjoy a different pace of life.* If I was going to live life unafraid no matter what, I had to let go of those expectations. This took time. Jesus was patient with me. He kept holding out his hands, and I kept putting pieces of my expectations into them. Piece by piece I dropped my expectations, my dreams into his hands: seeing the boys marry, grandchildren, retirement, dreams of seeing new places, long life.

As the expectations were released, Jesus filled the space with peace. Peace to accept my life as it comes, without the burden of expectations. And when the burden of expectations lifted, an acceptance grew within me. The fear of recurrence couldn't withstand the light of God's peace. Acceptance that my life is not mine, and God is truly in control. Acceptance that God knows my dreams, and his will for me is my best-case scenario.

In my Canadian culture there is a widely accepted idea suffering shouldn't be part of life.

All kinds of products are created to mitigate physical suffering. Commercialism promises that working towards attaining a certain lifestyle will eliminate any kind of suffering. The pandemic exposed the cracks in this philosophy. It brought issues of human connection to the forefront, forcing the culture to acknowledge relationships are a human need. The ultimate relationship that will fulfill us is with Jesus.

However, nowhere in Scripture does it promise a relationship with Jesus means the elimination of suffering. Jesus suffered through brutal torture and execution. In this time, he provided the perfect response to suffering. His acceptance of suffering acknowledged God's purposes are beyond human plans. While shouts for execution filled Jesus' ears, his mind focused resolutely on the purpose for the suffering.

Jesus knew suffering would be part of human existence. He experienced it firsthand. The teachings of Jesus are many, but the purpose is always the same, to point us to a relationship with God. In the Bible, we see a lot of talk about the grapevine. It had both economic and cultural value, making the grapevine central to everyday life. Jesus took this well-known plant and used it to teach us about what our relationship to God should really be like. In John 15, Jesus talks about being a vine, where we should remain. "I am the true grapevine, and my Father is the gardener. He cuts off every branch of mine that doesn't produce fruit, and he prunes the branches that do bear fruit so they will produce even more." (John 15:1-2, NLT) It's an interesting analogy, and one that would have been easy for his first century audience to relate to.

I had to ponder and reflect on the message of this analogy for my twenty-first century life. The amazing thing about the Bible is the message applies over time. I am living centuries after Jesus used this analogy, but it still carries profound meaning. If I am to think of my life as a branch, then the purpose is not mine to dictate. The branch doesn't dictate what kind of fruit is produced, the vine does. The branch doesn't give the source of nutrients needed to produce fruit, the vine does. The purpose of the fruit is not to sustain the branch. The purpose of the branch producing the fruit is to provide sustenance for others.

I had read this teaching of Jesus' many times, heard sermons on it, even participated in Bible studies about it. I understood the idea Jesus is our source. The part I struggled with in a cancer journey was the pruning. I felt like I had been serving God for a long time, and I could see fruit over the years. I knew I was connected to Jesus and he was the source for my life. This new season felt like the gardener had come along and pruned my life so severely there didn't appear to be anything left.

The suffering, mentally and physically, had been severe. My branch looked like there was nothing left in it. No hint of buds, no visible growth, just a bareness exposed to the elements. Pruning requires a sharp edge, and the pain of the process is real. We rarely speak of suffering in the pruning. It is a stripping away of ourselves. Once pruned, the branch has nothing left to do except wait. Wait for those life-giving nutrients to flow and create new growth.

The new growth happens around the cuts. The long-term benefits of pruning outweigh the immediate damage done. When you look closely at a pruned plant, you can see where the pruning took place. Around the area of the cuts is where the new growth sprouts. The gardener knows the damage caused by the cuts will produce a stronger and more fruitful branch. This doesn't mean that when God prunes our lives it isn't painful. God understands the suffering that accompanies the pruning. Jesus understands suffering in ways we can only scratch the surface of. He intimately understood my suffering. God didn't stop cancer from entering my body, from spreading, and becoming critical. What God did do is take the suffering and use it to demonstrate his power, his sovereignty, his ability to sustain. My response to suffering required a great deal of spiritual learning, waiting for the new growth to come. When growth happened, my spirit turned to acceptance of God and his will for my life, even if it meant suffering would be present.

A very beautiful thing began to happen after that. My sleep changed. As I prepared for bed, there wasn't emotional heaviness anymore. I wasn't just surviving each day, I was living, even thriving. The night was a chance to rest and allow the restorative power of sleep to do exactly what God designed it to do. The medication still interrupted some nights, but when I woke my mind was peaceful. The length of the sleepless periods decreased. Fear wasn't lurking in the corners of my mind anymore. Often when I woke, songs of praise were the first thing I thought of. The changes were a gift from God. The verse says, "because of you, Lord." Jesus provided an answer to my prayer. He taught me to trust him deeper, and our relationship grew. I was able to accept I didn't know where or how the journey would end. I could now trust Jesus would be enough for the journey, no matter what happened.

In my cancer journey, I have read the experiences of others, and I admire those who were brave enough to share their thoughts. I recognize the vulnerability required to share. The lessons others have learned were food for thought to me, something to ruminate on. As I read about the suffering of others, I came across an undercurrent. It wasn't always explicitly stated, but I uncovered a theme. So many who have been through a suffering journey expressed a thankfulness for the journey and what they learned. At first, I was shocked by this. *That's just crazy! No one should ever be thankful they got cancer!*

As I journeyed further down this road, I discovered what they were talking about. Being thankful for the journey doesn't mean you are thankful for the horrible things that happen. Being thankful for the journey means you are able to recognize where God has taken you in the suffering. My relationship with Jesus is far more intimate than before I got cancer. I don't ever want to lose that. Scripture has a much bigger place in my life, and I am sustained by it daily. I don't ever want to lose that. God has taught me how to listen to his voice, and I don't ever want to lose that. The need to know why has been replaced with a peaceful trust I recognize is a gift from a very loving God. My approach to every day focuses on how I can love God and love people. I don't ever want to lose that focus.

Can I throw things back at you for a moment? Suffering is not an isolated situation. Life is loaded with circumstances that bring suffering. Some of the circumstances are front and center, seen by all. Others are in the background and not easily recognized by those around us. Even though suffering is so pervasive there isn't a recipe to follow to get through it. Many times, we are unsure if we will even get through it. It skews our focus, demanding more energy than we have.

Are you dealing with a circumstance causing you suffering? You are not alone in this. Are you worn out with each step of the journey? Oh, how I understand that. Are you wondering what to do next? I don't have an easy recipe to follow, and I am not into pat answers. What I can offer you is not a formula to follow, but rather a person to follow. Jesus suffered. He understands suffering. He doesn't shrink back from the tough things. What he offers us is simple. He offers to walk with us in the suffering. When I allowed him to intimately join me in the suffering, he brought a strength to the journey beyond anything I could have imagined. That's the offer he has for you in your suffering. He is offering to be enough for you.

So, am I thankful for the journey? *Still working through that one!* Here is what I do know. I am thankful for where God has taken me in spite of horrible circumstances. That's what he offers. A chance to take any circumstance and be enough for it. *Jesus, you are enough for me!*

I will be still and know that you are God.

You are my refuge and strength, an ever-present help in trouble. Therefore, I will not fear.

But as for me, I will always have hope; I will praise you more and more.

I praise you, Lord, for being my guide. Even in the darkest night, your teachings fill my mind. I will keep my eyes always on the Lord. With him at my right hand I will not be shaken. Therefore, my heart is glad, and my tongue rejoices, and my body will also rest secure.

Though you have made me see troubles, many and bitter, you will restore my life again, from the depths of the earth you will again bring me up.

Lord, in all the challenges that lie ahead, help me to trust in you. My times are in your hands...Let your face shine on your servant; save me in your unfailing love. Let me not be put to shame Lord, for I have cried out to you.

Help me to give my entire attention to what you are doing right now, and not get worked up about what may or may not happen tomorrow. I claim the promise that God will help me deal with whatever hard things come up when the time comes.

Give me faith to not be afraid or discouraged for I believe the Lord will personally go ahead of me. He will be with me. He will neither fail me nor abandon me.

Oh God, spread your protection over me. Father, cover me with favor as with a shield.

So we're not giving up. How could we! Even though on the outside it often looks like things are falling apart on us, on the inside, where God is making new life, not a day goes by without His unfolding grace.

Now, because of you, Lord, I will lie down in peace, and sleep comes at once, for no matter what happens, I will live unafraid.

Chapter 12

Friendship... is born at the moment when
one says to another, "What! You too?
I thought that no one but myself..."
C.S. Lewis

Well my friend, that is my story. Can I call you friend? Maybe that's a little presumptuous on my part, but often friendship is forged out of shared experience. Reading this far, you know my journey and you have shared in the experiences. Thank you for the gift of your time with me. Often in sharing a journey with others we can find some benefit for ourselves. Shared experiences create connections.

I intended this writing to allow opportunity for others to feel a connection, to bridge the gap of isolation suffering brings. Life brings pain, heartache, grief, anguish. No one really escapes that. Life also brings opportunities for connection. We were not meant for isolation. God himself reached down and pursued us, just so there would be a relationship between him and us. When experiences and circumstances get heavy, we feel isolated. That's how the enemy of our soul works. We become convinced no one else understands, no one else experiences the same things, that we are all on our own. But that's exactly where God's plan roars in.

God desires to be in relationship with us. That desire was so strong he actively pursued us by sending Jesus. Jesus' sacrificial death once and for all took away the separation. Now God is as close as our next breath. He waits for you to recognize his presence and reach out. I know it's kind of scary. Many times in my journey I have realized I needed to trust God more, but also felt some fear. I learned that Jesus has never let me down. That's why I had to write my story out and share it with you. There's one more piece of my journey I want to share.

Ever walk down a long path and then turn around to see where you have come from? Reflecting can allow us to recognize things previously unseen and clarify our perspective. Many times I have been out for a run and found my breathing getting heavier, my leg muscles complaining more loudly. When I turn around and look back on the path, I can see the gradual incline I've been running. It was too gradual to immediately recognize, but the impact was still there, the effects apparent in my body. Focusing on the step immediately in front of me didn't allow me to recognize the challenge in the path. Only turning around and looking back allowed me to see clearly what I was up against. Lately, I have been doing some turning around, reflecting on where my cancer journey has taken me.

Part of this has been a forced reflection in order to write. You see, it's painful to look back and recognize everything I've been through. Writing forced a reflection that often included reliving the experiences. There were times where Keith happened upon me when I was writing, and I would be a total mess. A look of concern would overtake his face and he would ask what in the world was happening. I reassured him that I was just writing. After several of these instances happened, I tried to explain to him what was going on. As I wrote, I processed everything: the pain, the grief, the uncertainty, the assurances, the surrendering, and the peace. It has been a necessary part of healing.

My reflections led me back to something that happened at the beginning, while I was still in the hospital. The long days alone allowed for much time in quiet thought. Often, I would read my Bible and reflect. One of the stories I read shared the story of Jesus quieting a storm. It is found in Matthew, Mark, and Luke.[5] I had read the different versions to see the comparisons. I'd also listened to a sermon on the story to see what I could learn about being in a storm. I reflected on how the disciples must have been feeling. Their fear may have started small, but it grew to the point that it was paramount. Strong wind and mounting waves overwhelmed them. They feared for their lives.

I could totally relate to how the disciples felt. I was in a storm that threatened my life, and I was terrified. Words like brain tumor, craniotomy, and cancer were giant waves crashing into my life from all sides, swamping and threatening to sink me. I cried out to God in desperation. At that moment of deep fear, God gave me a vivid vision.

I saw myself in a boat with a huge storm around me. Wind was howling and waves crashed into the boat from all sides. As I looked around, I saw Jesus sitting in the front of the boat. He smiled at me and told me to come and sit with him, so I did. As I sat down, he wrapped me in his arms and covered us both with a blanket, right up over our heads so I couldn't see the storm. I could still hear the wind blowing and screeching. I could hear massive waves colliding against the boat. I experienced a strong sensation of being tossed around. Feeling all of that chaos, sitting in the arms of Jesus, I heard him speak to me. He told me I had to go through this storm, but we would ride it out together. I told him how scared I was, and he smiled, held me tight and told me he knew how scary this was for me. He told me to stay right there with him, and he was holding me, and would continue to keep me in his arms for the whole storm. I kept feeling the effects of the powerful storm outside of me, but slowly, I began to feel a calm within. It started small, just barely recognizable, but kept growing. I heard Jesus whispering over and over, "I'm here. Not going anywhere. I've got you in this."

Then my eyes opened, and I was still lying in a hospital bed. Activity bustled around me. I didn't feel like I was waking up from a dream. I was alert. My eyes roamed around the room. Still the same place. My ears took in the sounds of beeping monitors, quiet conversations, and beds being wheeled down the hall. *Yup, still here in the hospital.* The storm was still all around me, but I knew I also had something else—a profound confidence in God's presence. I knew I was being held in Jesus' arms every moment, every second. This brought peace in every fiber of my being. God announced he was enough, and that he would be enough for whatever was coming next.

Time has passed since I received that vision. Now the storm has calmed, and I've reached the other side. Jesus has gently led me up on the shore to continue my journey. When I think back to that vision, I clearly remember Jesus' message to me. I had to go through the storm. He wasn't going to calm this one like he did for the disciples that night. This storm would rage, and I would experience all the power a storm can bring. But I also had his promise to be with me through every part of it. This has been proven true. I can turn around now and see where Jesus was with me. I recognize his fingerprints over everything, I can see how he worked, the provision he gave, his presence in every minute. I had to go through the storm, but I was never alone, and he was always enough.

One of my favorite places to walk is a wooded area near my house. A few months back we experienced a derecho. This is a severe storm that includes thunderstorms and very high winds. It carves a fairly straight line of destruction that can be easily tracked. My first walk through the forest after the storm was sad. The damage to the woods was extensive. Trees down everywhere. Trees that had stood proudly, grown tall with wide trunks and long limbs, provided shade and beauty to the forest, had crashed over, their root system ripped out of the ground, totally exposed. I tracked the path of the severe wind by severed limbs, the forest rent and torn. Just so much damage. The whole landscape, forever altered.

The other day I was back in those same woods. At first I observed the damage, still readily evident. My focus was on what had been lost. As I trekked along, the sunlight caught my eye, and I began to notice something else. Downed trees allowed an increase in sunlight and new growth. Different plants flourished because light now reached new places. The storm had been severe, and damage had been done. But in the aftermath of that storm, there was opportunity for new growth.

Kind of like my life. Cancer was my storm. It had blown in, unexpected, harsh, and causing severe damage. Some of the loss was irreversible. I was forever altered physically, but the emotional damage was also evident. Some of the loss revealed where I had allowed my selfish desires to grow like a vine that wraps around a tree, preventing it from flourishing. My storm revealed where roots were shallow, not grounded in Jesus, but rather my own strength.

Now that the clouds have drifted off to the side, in the aftermath of the storm, I fully recognize the impact of the storm. I also notice something else though. There are areas where light is now able to get through. New opportunities are growing. I have to keep my head up and look around. If I keep my eyes on the ground right in front of me, things are dark and rough. But when I raise my head and look around at the whole picture, I see the new growth. God is creating something out of the storm. That's what he does. In Jesus, nothing is wasted. God is still writing my story.

Enough. We use the word enough in so many ways. I may push away from a celebratory meal, full of rich food, and exclaim "enough." My body has enough and the eating has to stop. Other times it is a command. When the arguments of our children reach our ears, perhaps for what seems like the millionth time, we raise our voices in protest, shouting "enough." The start of my cancer journey was full of these kinds of protests. I just wanted the suffering to stop. If I'm honest, I shouted "enough" many, many times along the way. It was protesting my circumstances.

I've changed my tone now. It didn't happen overnight. The process was incremental but steady. Each moment that I chose to trust Jesus, perspective shifted. Each surrender, with all of the struggle that entailed, brought an increasing peace. As I laid down each aspect of my life, there was nothing left of me. That's where the Holy Spirit moved in, taking up residence in every facet of my life.

God was so gracious, so loving in the journey. He guided gently, but firmly, never abandoning me. With the benefit of God's gracious strength and guidance in the journey, I can look back and raise my voice to proclaim "enough." I'm not protesting anymore, shouting "enough" to make things stop. I'm shouting "enough" to describe Jesus. I'm proclaiming that Jesus is enough. Full stop. End of sentence. He was and still remains enough. He is enough for the doubts, enough for the fear, enough for the questions, enough for the pain, enough for the weariness, enough for the uncertainty.

I have no idea what your journey is taking you through, what you have experienced in the past, or what might be lurking around the corner. You may be questioning why God took the person you loved so much to heaven. You may be questioning why the marriage ended. You may be fighting a battle with mental illness that is impacting you or a loved one. The job may have disappeared, or maybe someone important in your life has disappeared. Physical pain may be a daily reality. You may be dealing with the negative impact of someone else's choices. Life can be excruciatingly hard and leave us feeling helpless.

In those moments, when life's circumstances leave you shouting "enough" to try and make things stop, there is hope. Jesus brings hope into every circumstance. His strength is enough for weakness, his peace is enough for fear and uncertainty, his presence is enough for confusion, his comfort is enough for heartache. I'm not making these statements lightly. Putting complete trust in Jesus can be a hard-fought process. We have an enemy who does not want you to give any portion of your trust away. He will fight you every step, raise doubt and fears that seem insurmountable. What I have learned is this. Every time I put my trust in Jesus, he was enough. Every time I surrendered myself, my fear, my pain, he was enough. Every time I looked up from the dark path, I saw that he was with me, giving enough light for me to take another step. He never failed me. He is waiting to do that for you if you will put your trust in him.

I'm here today to tell you God is enough for whatever is going on in your life. I'm proclaiming loudly, "Enough!" because Jesus is enough for anything, and I want everyone to know.

God's Word proclaims he is enough. Each of these verses are a treasured word God spoke to me on my journey. Together they form a prayer that is a foundation as I continue this life with Jesus.

I encourage you to pray with me:

Oh Jesus,

I will be still and know that you are God.

You are my refuge and strength, an ever-present help in trouble. Therefore, I will not fear.

But as for me, I will always have hope; I will praise you more and more.

I praise you Lord for being my guide. Even in the darkest night, your teachings fill my mind. I will keep my eyes always on you Lord. With Jesus at my right hand, I will not be shaken. Therefore, my heart is glad, and my tongue rejoices, and my body will also rest secure.

Though you have made me see troubles, many and bitter, you will restore my life again, from the depths of the earth you will again bring me up.

Lord, in all the challenges that lie ahead, help me to trust in you. My times are in your hands. Let your face shine on your servant; save me in your unfailing love. Let me not be put to shame Lord, for I have cried out to you.

Help me to give my entire attention to what you are doing right now, and not get worked up about what may or may not happen tomorrow. I claim the promise that God will help me deal with whatever hard things come up when the time comes.

Give me faith to not be afraid or discouraged, for I believe you will personally go ahead of me. You will be with me. You will neither fail me nor abandon me.

Oh God, spread your protection over me. Oh God, cover me with your favor as with a shield.

Father, I am not giving up. How could I! Even though on the outside it often looks like things are falling apart, on the inside, where you are making new life, not a day goes by without your unfolding grace.

Now, because of you Lord, I will lie down in peace, and sleep comes at once, for no matter what happens, I will live unafraid.

In Jesus' name, Amen.

Endnotes

1. Genesis 3

2. Oxford Languages. Oxford University Press, ©2023

3. The Science of Emotion: Exploring the Basics of Emotional Psychology(Posted June 27, 2019 by UWA/*Psychology and Counseling News*)

4. Ephesians 6:10-20

5. Matthew 8:23-27, Mark 4:35-41, Luke 8:22-25

www.ingramcontent.com/pod-product-compliance
Lightning Source LLC
Chambersburg PA
CBHW071306030726
47594CB00002B/337